A Geographia Guide

Northern Scotland

with the Orkneys
Shetlands and Hebrides

INCLUDING

FALKIRK
STIRLING
ST. ANDREWS
PERTH
ARRAN
OBAN
FORT WILLIAM
DUNDEE
ABERDEEN
ELGIN
INVERNESS
SKYE
KIRKWALL
LERWICK

ISBN 0 09 205470 6

Guide to Northern Scotland
© Geographia Ltd.,
63 Fleet Street,
London, E.C.4.

Compiled and published by
Geographia Ltd.

Original Text: H. O. Wade

Line illustrations: W. Balmain

Photographic illustrations
British Tourist Authority

Series Editor: J. T. Wright

Made and printed in Great Britain by
The Anchor Press Ltd.,
Tiptree, Essex

Contents

Illustrations

Front Cover: Glencoe, Argyllshire
Back Cover: The Alexander Selkirk (Robinson Crusoe) Statue,
Lower Largo

Photographs:

Drawings:

Town Plans:

Every reasonable care has been taken to ensure that the information in this Guide is correct at the time of going to press. Nevertheless, the Publishers can accept no responsibility for errors or omissions or for changes in the details quoted.

Section 1   Introduction

The area covered by this Guide extends from the narrow waist of Scotland, clearly marked today by the Edinburgh–Glasgow motorway, northwards to the wild and broken coastline of Caithness and Sutherland; it includes the Orkneys and Shetlands as well as the Inner and Outer Hebrides.

Although new administrative boundaries became operative from May 1975, the traditional county names are used throughout this Guide. Current boundaries and names may be seen on the map inside the back cover.

Contrary to popular conception Northern Scotland does not all consist of Highlands, nor are the inhabitants all Highlanders. Three separate races have contributed to the present population, the original Picts, the Painted People; the Scandinavians, the Vikings and their more peaceful colonists who followed these pirates of the Long Ships; and the Scots from Northern Ireland. For the purpose of distinguishing between the various peoples that have contributed to the present somewhat varied population, the country may be divided into four sections. The east coast right around to Inverness and inland to the slopes of the Grampians is dominated by the Scandinavian element decreasing towards the inland regions. The west coast, including the islands of Argyllshire, but not the Hebrides, are essentially Gaelic. North of the Great Glen, in the wildest and most remote parts of the Highlands, the population is dominated by the Gaelic with a greater Scandinavian influence towards the north. Caithness and the eastern areas of Sutherland are largely Scandinavian in origin while the Orkneys, Shetlands and the Hebrides are almost entirely derived from the Northmen or Scandinavians. Throughout all these areas there is, of course, a greater or lesser mixture of both races. While the Gaelic tongue is spoken only in the west the Scots has crept, and still is, fast creeping, westwards largely because the Celt or Gael is the more adept at adopting fresh speech and cultures.

Geographically Northern Scotland may be divided as we have done in compiling this Guide. The northern parts of the great Edinburgh–Glasgow conurbation, Dumbarton, Stirling. Clackmannan, Fife and Kinross, although largely composed of somewhat flat farmlands, these counties all touch the hills and mountains to a greater or lesser extent. It is from the ramparts of Stirling Castle that the visitor obtains his first view of the still distant, but immensely impressive, mountains of the Southern Highlands to the north and west.

The semi-lowland coastal strip, which in places extends many miles inland, is largely good farming land with a wealth of rivers flowing from the Grampians and the Cairngorms, including many of Scotland's highest peaks, to the North Sea.

Banffshire, Moray and Nairn again consist of excellent agricultural land along the flat coastal strip backed by low hills with the Grampians and Cairngorms not far away and in clear view from any high spot.

The Highlands south of the Great Glen, including the islands of Argyllshire, and the Highlands north of the Great Glen with the Hebridean Islands are two areas among the wildest and most beautiful in Northern Scotland but each has very distinct scenery and characteristics of its own; each must of necessity be explored separately.

For the archaeologist there is a wealth of subject matter, especially in the north-east and in the Orkneys and Shetlands. The whole country is lavishly spread with ancient castles and the ruined remains of the Clans and the Clan system which was, perhaps, the greatest tragedy in Scottish history. Many of General Wade's roads can still be followed by the walker or the historian while several forts remain as subjects for study.

There are numbers of fine holiday resorts both large and small; the mountains and lochs with the endless succession of glens, a combination which only Scotland has to offer the visitor, make of Northern Scotland a playground for all where holidays can be enjoyed in individual style, in the surroundings most suited to our many varied likes and dislikes. When visiting Northern Scotland remember that a Scot is a Scot and not a Britisher; he is hospitable and friendly but above all a Scot.

HOW TO GET THERE

By Rail: Northern Scotland is surprisingly well catered for by British Railways. From Edinburgh or Glasgow there is a first-rate service along the east coast via Dundee and Aberdeen to Inverness. An excellent service via Stirling and Perth serves the same area. From Perth, with through trains from Edinburgh, there is a good service through magnificent country to Dunkeld, Pitlochry, Blair Atholl, Dalwhinnie, Newtonmore, Kingussie, Aviemore (the ski centre) and Carr Bridge to Inverness. This route takes the visitor through or alongside some of the highest mountain country.

From Inverness there is a not very frequent service to Thurso and Wick. Also a service to the Kyle of Lochalsh. Thurso is the port from which sail the steamers to Orkney. From Kyle of Lochalsh there is a continuous ferry service to Skye.

From Glasgow starts one of the world's most remarkable railway runs through some of the most beautiful country in the Highlands. This line runs alongside Loch Lomond to Arrochar and Tarbet, then to Crianlarich, where one line heads west for Oban while the other makes a never-to-be-forgotten journey through the Bridge of Orchy, Rannoch and Spean Bridge to Fort William, where a change is made for the spectacular run to Mallaig.

Local services around Edinburgh and Glasgow are excellent.

By Air: Regular services are flown from London and the Midlands to Edinburgh, Glasgow, Aberdeen and Wick. A daily service connects Wick with Kirkwall in the Orkneys and Lerwick in the Shetlands. Many of the Western Isles are served by air from Glasgow.

By Bus: The visitor will be surprised by the nature of the roads over which the companies operate a very good service indeed. All over the Highlands and the larger Islands there are bus services, some frequent, some very infrequent. On the west coast a great many inaccessible places are safely and reliably reached by bus. Enquiries about any individual service should be made through the major bus companies in Edinburgh, Glasgow or the centre where the visitor is staying.

By Sea to The Islands: Most of the Western Isles are served by the McBrayne line of steamers, comfortable, well-equipped boats. The main ports of embarkment are as follows: Gourock for Arran; Inveraray and Tarbert for Islay, Jura and Colonsay; Oban for Mull, Iona, Staffa, Coll and Tiree; Mallaig for Rum, Eigg, Muck, Canna and Barra; Kyle of Lochalsh for Skye and the Inner and Outer Hebrides. Most of these embarkation ports are themselves connected by steamer.

The Orkneys and Shetlands are well served from Leith, Aberdeen and Thurso. Each section of this Guide will contain some details of the transport to and from the places mentioned.

By Road: Northern Scotland will be found to have some of the best roads in the United Kingdom. Many of the minor roads, more especially in the Highlands, are single track with passing places, ideal for the motorist who desires a rest. From Edinburgh the new Forth Road Bridge will carry the motorist quickly to the Tay Bridge for Dundee and Aberdeen, or to Perth, there to take any one of five roads fanning out from south-west to north-east. All the important towns can be reached quickly. A journey up the east coast is a straight-forward run, a journey up the west coast is far more interesting and exciting; owing to the long sea lochs many miles have often to be motored to reach a place that can be seen across the loch with the naked eye. For the motorist the main road centres are Stirling, Perth, Aberdeen, Inverness, Fort William and Crianlarich.

The Geology of Northern Scotland

By Dr. D. A. Robson

The rocks which outcrop along the coast of the north-west Highlands are among the most ancient on the surface of the earth, dating back over 2,000 million years. These rocks, known as the Lewisian Gneiss, also form much of the land of the Outer Hebrides. In ancient times they made up a great continent across the region now occupied by the Atlantic ocean.

In those times this ancient continent was mountainous, and great rivers flowed eastwards from it, pouring their debris of sand over the shallow waters which occupied the present area of north-western Scotland. In this way, a considerable thickness of sand accumulated on top of the Lewisian Gneiss, and eventually it became indurated to form what is today described as the Torridon Sandstone. This sandstone can be seen on the Isles of Skye, Rhum and Islay, while on the mainland it forms the mountain masses of Torridon, Coigach, Cul Beag, Cul More and others, together with the impressive peaks of Suilven and Stac Polly.

Both the Lewisian Gneiss and the Torridonian rocks belong to the Pre-Cambrian era, and the great Atlantic continent persisted throughout the succeeding era, known as the Palaeozoic. Sand and mud, borne by the rivers from this continent, continued to pour into the subsiding trough which now extended over Scotland and northern England. These sediments accumulated to build a succession many thousands of feet thick. The earliest of these deposits, the Cambrian Quartzite, a pure white sandstone, can be seen capping some of the Torridon mountains. A somewhat later deposit, the Durness Limestone, can be followed from the north coast southwards through Assynt down to the latitude of Skye.

Towards the end of Lower Palaeozoic times, Scotland and northern England became the centre of earth-movements. The soft layered rocks, which had been accumulating in the subsiding trough from the end of Pre-Cambrian times, were thrust westwards and upwards against the Lewisian and Torridonian. They were fractured, folded over one another and metamorphosed (changed by heat and pressure) to form a mountain mass comparable in height with the Alps of the present day. The classical area in which to see these rocks is at Assynt, north of Ullapool, though the intense earth-movements affected the whole of northern Scotland, forming the North-West, the West and the Central Highlands.

In the wake of the earth-movements there occured great intrusions, or upwellings of molten material from the depths of the earth, into the rocks of the Highlands; they were accompanied by volcanic outbursts in western Argyll, in the Ochils, Sidlaws and elsewhere. The intrusions came to rest below the surface, but they have been exposed by erosion of the overlying strata in many cases. The huge peak of granite known as Ben Cruachan, in Argyll, marks the site of one of these intrusions, while the precipices of Glen Coe and the summit of Ben Nevis itself are of rock poured out by the volcanoes of those days.

Meanwhile the new land-mass of the Highlands now began to be eroded by river torrents which cascaded off the high ground towards the southern plain. Thick deposits of Highland boulders, pebbles and sand were spread out by these torrents and these deposits were interspersed by lava flows. Other torrents poured material into the depressions covering the regions now occupied by the Orkney Islands and the Moray Firth. All these deposits became hardened to form what is now known as the Old Red Sandstone. Remnants of this group of rocks may be seen all across Scotland between the Forth/Clyde line and the Highland border, as well as in the Moray and Orkney regions.

A further series of earth-movements rent Scotland some 100 million years after those which had created the Highlands. But these were more moderate and were confined to a certain number of long straight fractures trending north-east to south-west across the Highlands. Many of these fractures can today be recognised as long, deep depressions, often containing the waters of a loch. The most important of these fractures are the Highland Boundary fault and the Great Glen fault. The latter runs from the west to the east coasts, along the line of Loch Linnhe, Loch Lochy and Loch Ness. Geologists estimate that along this line the north of Scotland was moved in a south-westerly direction, by a whole series of earthquakes, over a total distance of about sixty-five miles.

Whereas the movement along the Great Glen was mainly horizontal, that along the Highland Boundary fault was chiefly vertical, with the rocks having been dropped down on the south side. This accounts for the sudden change in the character of the countryside, from Lowland to Highland, on adjacent sides of the fault. This change can be seen all along the Highland line, from the Isle of Arran to Stonehaven; the towns of Callander and Crieff lie immediately south of this line.

A much later series of events took place about fifty million years ago over the western part of Scotland, namely an immense outpouring of lava flows from volcanoes situated somewhere off what is now the west coast. Large remnants of these lavas are still visible today, forming much of the isles of Skye, Eigg and Mull, and the smaller isles of Canna, Muck and Staffa. In the latter, the lava pillars of Fingal's Cave are reminiscent of the Giant's Causeway in Northern Ireland.

Most recently the onset of the great Ice Age, which terminated about 10,000 years ago, had a profound effect upon the Highlands of Scotland. Glaciers developed at the head of the mountain valleys, where they carved out the corries; deep depressions were scoured out as the rivers of ice moved downhill. Enormous deposits of moraine (mixtures of boulders and sand) were laid down where the glaciers melted, as for example across the Moor of Rannoch. All the high mountain ridges were sharpened by the long-sustained action of frost. At the present time, there are no glaciers in Scotland, but snow often lingers in the shaded, north-facing corries until July. Had Ben Nevis been 1,000 feet higher, there would today have been glaciers on its flanks.

The Wildlife of Northern Scotland

By W. Balmain

Northern Scotland may be regarded as a last outpost for the vanishing wildlife of the British Isles. The remote vastness of mountains, a multitude of islands and depopulation of the Highlands have combined to allow a few species, which otherwise would surely now be extinct in our islands, to linger on.

In an area so vast it is impossible to summarise every species, and therefore to touch on the more rare and typical animals and birds is perhaps the best approach.

Scotland has some 173,000 acres of National Nature Reserve, islands unique in the world, and moorland and highlands which although altered by the hand of man can now be said to afford some semblance of hope where not so very many years ago complete spoilation seemed inevitable.

Man's destruction of the natural forests has had perhaps the greatest effect. The Vikings began it in A.D. 800 by burning, and felling trees to build their boats. Thereafter it continued through the centuries whenever clearances were needed to make grazing-grounds for livestock, for building purposes and industrial interests and during wars.

Now reafforestation by conifers is providing a second-best alternative to the old mixed woodlands.

Some species of wildlife now well established, were once indeed extinct. The reintroduction of the capercaillie is a prime example of repopulation. Reindeer experimentally introduced are thriving well in Glenmore. Ptarmigan, mountain hares and the golden eagle linger on whilst the Scottish wild cat and pine marten are now making a remarkable comeback. The pine marten's spread, as well as that of the Scottish crossbill, greater spotted woodpecker, raven, roedeer, red squirrel, and other species of birds and animals, may be directly attributed to reafforestation.

Red deer stalk the deep glens and mountain ranges, red and black grouse are found in great numbers across the moorlands. The peregrine still reigns as queen of the hunting falcons. Together with hosts of wildfowl such comparative rarities as the red-throated diver and slavonian grebe frequent the waters. The return of the osprey as a breeding bird to Scotland has been one of the great occasions in recent times for naturalists.

Whooper swans are found in great numbers on the many lochs in wintertime, but it is to the islands we must go for truly impressive wildlife records.

St. Kilda has become the greatest gannetry in the world, and N. Rona affords breeding grounds for one-seventh of the world's population of grey seals. Hebridean sheep, once the native breed found throughout the West Highlands and Islands, may still be seen on St. Kilda. Dark-fleeced, some with four horns, these soays are now an interesting relic from the past. The island of Rhum is almost an open-air laboratory with 26,400 acres famous for its herds of red deer. Guillemot, razorbill and puffin are common to most island cliffs, waders are seen in hundreds on every shore. Fulmars, once the staple food of many islanders, are increasing at a rapid rate.

Buzzards range over the lonely moors and feral goats seen occasionally on the hills have reverted to their wild state. Otters still hunt the mountain burns and badgers are reportedly on the increase.

Off the shores basking sharks, ray and skate are seen, whilst migrant whales sometimes frequent West Highland and Hebridean coasts. Killer whales harry the common and grey seal.

Although the wolf, bear, lynx, lemming, beaver, elk and other creatures are gone from these regions for ever, some say the polecat may still exist in the Highlands. It is the birds to whom we must look for recolonisation : they have the mobility to reach Scotland from other lands if conditions prove favourable to them again. Certainly the law and attitude towards wildlife are changing but one wonders what effect the vogue of syndicated sport will have.

Motoring in Northern Scotland

The average motorist must surely find that Northern Scotland is the land of endless and varying opportunity. Here there are long straight stretches with less traffic than the southerner is accustomed to, twisting hilly sections that will test his skill to the full. And here the motorist looking for peace and quiet will find miles and miles of roadway with excellent surface and little traffic where quiet motoring becomes almost a habit within a few days.

The greatest joy of the roads of Northern Scotland is the number of lay-bys, the wide road verges and other places where the motorist can pull off the road to enjoy the scenery or to camp for a night or two. Peace and a welcome seem to pervade the atmosphere.

Perth is perhaps the greatest motoring centre above Edinburgh–Glasgow ; here seven roads fan out taking the motorist to Aberdeen via Dundee, via Forfar or via Braemar To Inverness via

Aviemore or Braemar. Through Pitlochry to Inverness or westwards
to Fort William. Another glorious road is through Crieff and the
Bridge of Orchy to Fort William. Lastly there is the gentler road to
Dunblane and The Trossachs. The route through Braemar from Perth
follows the beautiful Glenshee and negotiates the Devil's Elbow
which will test the skill of any young motorist. From Braemar to
Inverness involves a stretch of secondary road that for hill scenery is
hard to beat on this, the east, side of Scotland.

Within a few miles of Inverness the motorist headed north gets
the same choice of routes with a number of secondary roads that
generally seem to pass through the pick of the scenery. From the
most north-westerly point at Durness the motorist will find but little
choice on his journey south ; however, there are side roads that make
for more adventurous and very uncrowded motoring.

In Orkney and Shetland there is, of course, little choice of route,
but all the more important, and many of the unimportant, islands have
good, if narrow motor roads. Exactly the same may be said of all the
Western Isles. The ferry services are good and the welcome assured.
While the garages and service stations are more plentiful than many
would suppose there are a few long stretches of road where a full
tank is advisable.

For the caravanner this is ideal country, plenty of room and good
individual parking sites almost everywhere, by lochside and burn, on
the hills and in the glens. There is always room for camper or
caravanner.

Walking in Northern Scotland

For the keen walker Northern Scotland must represent something
rather special as a walking terrain. It is not generally realised that
Scotland has no law of trespass ; in England one may be obliged
to keep to the footpaths and can be evicted on refusal. In Scotland
the walker can walk any where so long as no damage is done. If this
advantage is utilised with good common sense and respect for the
other man's property it opens up whole new worlds to the walker.
Obey the Country Code and you will find that you are welcome to
walk the hills and glens at will.

For the professional the west coast from north to south is the ideal
stamping ground where map and compass are a necessity, where
even with these aides difficulty can often be experienced owing to
the lochs, both sea and land lochs, to the upthrusts of rock intrusions
and forests. All these difficulties make of any long-distance
cross-country walk in the western or northern Highlands an exercise
in the use of the skills and care that together constitute the difference
between the professional and the amateur.

For the beginner in this most natural of man's recreations the
well-known glens and the loch-side walks are recommended ; there

are also, of course, well-known and much used footpaths where the chance of getting lost is fairly remote. Always take a 1 in. O.S. map and a compass, use them and thereby gain the practise that will enable you to walk the unmarked hills and the wild and sparsely populated country of the west and north. Remember always to travel properly and warmly clad, in trousers not shorts, with weather-proofs in the rucksack and wearing heavy weather-proof boots. Always carry food and a hot drink or a spirit stove, water can almost always be easily found; carry a torch and a whistle. All these things are vitally necessary should you become lost in a mist, should you twist an ankle or become ill. And, finally, plan your walk and tell someone of your route and expected time of arrival; thus those who give up their time to look for you will know just what line to take and your torch and whistle will attract attention.

Many of General Wade's roads are still in existence and many of his bridges are still there although only a few are in use. These roads and the finding of them constitute one of the great interests in walking. In the following pages many of these roads will be mentioned and the most easily accessible points noted. There are other old roads, drove roads in particular, which can be the venue for a most interesting day or longer period.

When walking in Northern Scotland treat the country and the Scots with respect—you will be welcomed. If you need help or information ask for it, the Scot is a kindly and hospitable being but very independent, as becomes the descendants of the proud and warlike Clans of not so long ago.

By the shores of Loch Lomond

Section 2 South of the Highlands

Edinburgh

Edinburgh occupies an enviable position as the capital of one of the most beautiful countries in the northern hemisphere. It is the spiritual home of the, often tragic, history of Scotland and, without doubt, it is the most impressive city in the British Isles.

For the visitor by train or by car Princes Street is the first and most impressive sight of this very beautiful city that he or she will get; and since first impressions are often lasting most people remember Edinburgh as Princes Street. The south side is completely taken up with the glorious gardens, the Scott Monument and the Castle on its rugged hill-top. The north side is occupied by handsome buildings and shops; women will find Edinburgh a first-class shopping centre.

Edinburgh started life before the Romans arrived as a few primitive dwellings on the volcanic plug upon which later on the castle was built. Around this it grew until in the middle eighteenth century modern Edinburgh was planned and built; this consisted of Queen Street, George Street and Princes Street. Industrially the city grew along the river front and remains so today.

Among the many important, beautiful and impressive sights the visitor should not miss are the following. Princes Street with its gardens and the Scott Monument. Edinburgh Castle including the eleventh-century St. Margaret's Chapel, the very moving Scottish War Memorial and the Crown Room containing the Scottish Regalia, Crown, Sceptre, Sword of State, etc. The nearby Outlook Tower which houses an exhibition of Scottish Life through the centuries. The Palace of Holyroodhouse. The Royal Mile (detailed in *Southern Scotland*). St. Giles Cathedral noted as the High Kirk of Edinburgh and the very heart of Scotland.

In addition there are nearly a dozen museums and art collections, a wealth of churches and some old buildings with a great historic interest. Edinburgh is rich in theatres and cinemas as well as cultural activities of all kinds.

Glasgow

As compared to Edinburgh, Glasgow is a very young city indeed. It was not until 1172 that King William the Lion granted a charter to Bishop Jocelyn to found a Bishop's Burg on the banks of the

Molendiner Burn and the right to hold a market on Thursdays. Thus started the city that today is large enough to contain the three big cities of Edinburgh, Dundee and Aberdeen with room to spare. The deep water River Clyde is, of course, the reason for the immense growth and prosperity of Glasgow.

Last century it was said that anything manufactured anywhere in the world was also manufactured in Glasgow; this is not now true if it ever was; it would, however, surprise the visitor to see a complete list of industrial activities of this riverside city so near the sea. Ship-building, exports and imports, as they always have, still dominate the industrial scene.

The poverty and the residue of the industrial revolution are being cleared away, but this is a long task; a lot has been done and Glasgow can today boast sixty-one public parks, eighty-one children's playgrounds, one thousand ornamental spaces and a Country Park near Loch Lomond; in addition Glasgow has part of the National Park in Argyllshire.

From a cultural point of view Glasgow is one of the chief centres of Scotland with a wealth of theatres, cinemas, museums, exhibitions and cultural activities of every sort.

Glasgow would hardly be counted a holiday resort yet every visitor to Northern Scotland should visit this city that has so much to show. One of the most impressive entrances to Glasgow is by sea; past Ailsa Craig, not far from the beautiful Island of Arran, close alongside that delightful stretch of coast on the south bank of the Firth of Clyde, from Greenock to Gourock and Port Glasgow, with the wooded greenery of Dunbartonshire to the north. This is the age-old entrance to Glasgow and is still by far the finest and most impressive. For those who wish to explore Glasgow more closely there is a somewhat more detailed survey in the *Geographia Guide to Southern Scotland.*

The Edinburgh–Glasgow Industrial Area

The largely industrial area extending from the Edinburgh–Glasgow motorway to a line drawn roughly from Falkirk through Kirkintilloch to Dumbarton is not of great interest to the holiday visitor; however, there are a number of places that should be seen, for much of this particular area is extremely beautiful and throughout there are historical relics, lovely old churches and places of great interest.

Only a few miles from Edinburgh and very close to South Queensferry is the very lovely little Church of St. Cuthbert's at Dalmeny village, which has the distinction of being the most completely Norman church in Scotland; rebuilding of certain parts has taken place from time to time but the original design has been adhered to throughout. There are signs that the masons who built this church were also responsible for Dunfermline Abbey. Of twelfth-century origin the walls and a great deal more are original.

The Royal and Ancient Burgh of Queensferry, now known as South Queensferry, is one of those very pleasant little places that keeps its own identity in spite of the overpowering effect of the two great bridges. From several parts of the town some truly magnificent views can be obtained. The Hawes Brae is the termination of the first turnpike road in Scotland. There are many fine old buildings of which the most famous is probably the Carmelite Priory Church, the only medieval Carmelite church still in use in the country.

Near South Queensferry are several ancient castles which are well worth a visit. Niddry Castle is the one to which Mary Queen of Scots escaped from her prison on Loch Leven. Little seems to be known of Dundas Castle but the village and Castle of Blackness have an interesting history; the Castle is under the care of the Dept. of Environment and is open to the public. Its age is not known but in the fifteenth century it was considered of importance in the defence of Scotland. Standing on a spit of rock jutting into the waters of the Firth of Forth it has a most sinister appearance.

A short distance south of Blackness is one of the most interesting houses in West Lothian, The Binns, a National Trust property and open to the public at certain times. The oldest parts of the present most impressive house date from before 1478 while the site has probably been inhabited since before the Normans arrived. The Royal Scots Greys were raised at The Binns in 1681 by General Tam Dalyell. A member of the Dalyell family still lives at this quite ancient and very beautiful house.

LINLITHGOW. Population approx. 5,000

Linlithgow, the county town of West Lothian, is a Royal Burgh and is distinguished by several fine and ancient buildings which warrant more than a cursory glance. It is also distinguished as the birthplace of Mary Queen of Scots. The town itself is blessed with a pleasant atmosphere and some quite beautiful old buildings that have lost a good deal of their charm by reason of the nearby ultra-modern erections. However, the great glory of Linlithgow is the Palace and the Church of St. Michael's.

St. Michael's is considered one of the finest examples of Gothic architecture in Scotland. It dates from the thirteenth century and stands on the site of an earlier church. Both inside and outside this is a church that should not be missed by lovers of the fine architecture of the past. The fine square tower has been surmounted, in 1965, by a symbolism of the crown of thorns; this is in gold laminated wood and completely spoils the outside appearance unless the visitor refrains from looking upwards. Apart from this one point, a purely modern conception, this is one of the loveliest churches in Scotland.

The Palace of Linlithgow is undoubtedly one of the glories of Scottish architecture, and to quote that great authority on the architecture of Scotland, W. Douglas Simpson, 'is beyond doubt the most purposeful piece of planning in the whole range of old Scottish domestic architecture'. Building was commenced by James I in 1425 and completed in 1539. Today it is a shell only but complete as to its walls, and a very great deal of the very fine and noble decorative architecture is clearly visible. The Palace stands at the head of a great green park sloping down to the loch and altogether makes not only a noble picture but a very fine park which the public are able to enjoy under the control of the Dept. of Environment.

Linlithgow has always been famous for its wells. The names of some of the Wynds bear this out: the Dog Well Wynd, the New Well Wynd and St. Michael's Well which still bears the motto 'St. Michael's is kinde to strangers'. The Town House in the Cross is another building especially worth a visit.

Between Linlithgow and Queensferry is Hopetoun House, the home of the Marquess of Linlithgow and one of the largest and most elegant of Scottish Georgian houses; it was begun in 1696 and completed in 1703; some twenty years later it was enlarged and somewhat redesigned. Since the middle 1700s the house and the extremely beautiful grounds and gardens have remained virtually unaltered. The house and grounds are open to the public at certain times in the summer months.

Close to the shores of the Firth of Forth and not far from Hopetoun House is one of the most fairylike villages to be found anywhere, Abercorn, a relic of the last century with a situation to fit. The few houses are grouped around the old church with the date 1612. The churchyard is beautifully kept and the whole village shows the loving care of the few inhabitants. The situation is in woodland which adds to the beauty and prevents outside noise from interfering with the sylvan setting.

A little south of Linlithgow is a small range of hills known as the Bathgate Hills. Fairly heavily wooded, these hills provide a happy and beautiful playground for the teeming population of Edinburgh and district. There are several quiet roads which afford some fine views, while pony trekking is becoming popular and footpaths make walking an easy and pleasurable pastime. These hills are very similar, on a smaller scale, to the Pentlands.

Cairnpapple Hill, three miles north of Bathgate, was the scene in 1947–8 of a discovery of great importance when Pictish remains were uncovered, including stone implements of several kinds dating from 2000–3000 B.C. The excavations are under the control of the Dept. of Environment. The quite short climb is well worth while for the grand view. This is one of the highest points in the Bathgate Hills.

About ten miles from Edinburgh on the Stirling road is the village of Kirkliston, with a twelfth-century church. This is one of the gems of the many ancient churches in this part of Scotland.

CUMBERNAULD. Population approx. 28,000

Cumbernauld is a brand new and very modern town built to relieve Glasgow's overspill. It has first-class transport by road, rail and air and in every sense is the ultra-modern industrial town and dormitory.

KIRKINTILLOCH. Population approx. 24,000

Kirkintilloch was anciently in the Barony of Cumbernauld and was a Burgh or Barony in the time of William the Lion; the charter is dated at Forres on 2 October; the year was not mentioned but is assumed to have been 1214 and so the Town Council celebrated their seven hundred and fiftieth anniversary in 1964. The Roman Antonine Wall ran right through what is now the town, and in Peel Park is the site of the Roman Fort. It is believed that the Picts had a settlement here. Old St. Mary's Church at the Cross is the only building of age in the town, it was erected in 1644 and although somewhat rebuilt in 1956 it remains a very handsome and quite beautiful edifice. There was a church erected in 1140 by Thorald of the Barony of Kirkintilloch and Cumbernauld; an archway and belfry built from the stones of this church are all that remain; they stand at the entrance to the burial ground.

AIRDRIE AND COATBRIDGE

Both these towns are in Lanarkshire and both are purely industrial. They are however both very pleasant and first class examples of the Scottish industrial community that is clearing away the poverty and residue of the industrial revolution and the Victorian era as well as the havoc wrought by the 'thirties'. Both have their attractions but not of the kind to draw the holidaymaker. As examples of twentieth century town development they are well worthy of a visit.

CLYDEBANK. Population approx. 50,000

Although Clydebank is virtually a part of Greater Glasgow it deserves a few words on account of its quite unusual history and its phenomenally rapid growth. Today it is of course almost entirely industrial but includes some lovely parks and is close to country of great beauty and attractiveness.

Merely a hundred years ago this was all agricultural land peopled by Burns's 'Ploughman and Reaper'. Travelling along the old turnpike road in those days one would have seen only the Firth of Clyde to the south and the fields to the north backed by the Kilpatrick Hills and the Forth and Clyde canal. It was in 1871 that George and James Thomson moved their shipbuilding yards to Clydebank; these later became the world famous yards of John Brown. Other firms followed and Clydebank grew apace.

Overtoun Park is one of the loveliest and many other features of the new Clydebank are most attractive. Railway and bus services are first rate while Glasgow Airport is no great distance away.

Dumbarton

Status: Burgh.
How to Get There: (*By Rail*). Excellent train service from Glasgow to three stations in Dumbarton.
(*By Road.*) Good bus service from Glasgow and area, connections to all important centres by coach.
Population: 25,470.
Early Closing Day: Wednesday.
Post Office: 35 College Way.
Tourist Information Office: Town Clerk's Office.
Places of Worship: Dumbarton Riverside Parish Church, St. Augustine's Episcopal Church, St. Patrick's R.C. Church.
Parking Places: Quay Street, College Street, Station Road, Town Centre Redevelopment Area.
Cinema: Rialto, College Street.
Theatres: Denny Civic Theatre, Town Centre, Dumbarton People's Theatre, Glasgow Road.
Parks and Open Spaces: Levengrove Park.
Newspapers: Lennox Herald and County Reporter (Friday and Wednesday).
Other Amenities: Angling, golf, indoor baths, tennis. A considerable cultural activity.

THE ROAD FROM Glasgow to Dumbarton is largely industrialised and of little interest to the holidaymaker. The A811 follows the Clyde through Clydebank to join the A82 very close to the site of Dunglass Castle. Another two miles brings the visitor into the quite pleasant industrial Burgh of Dumbarton.

Although not a holiday resort there are several things of real interest to be seen. Dumbarton Castle is more than worth a visit on its 240-foot rock which since ancient times has dominated the town and the pass to Loch Lomond. The Rock has two summits—one is topped by the Castle and the other by an ancient Watch Tower and a view indicator. Both should be visited for the splendid views. The Rock stands at the junction of the River Leven and the Clyde; the pool beneath was for many centuries the Port for Dumbarton. Greit House, now a gas showroom and shop, was built in 1623 and is the most distinguished building in Dumbarton. The Municipal Buildings in the Scottish Baronial style are well worth viewing. On the west side of the River Leven is the delightful little park of Levengrove, and while still on the west side of the Leven there is Castle Hill, the property of the National Trust for Scotland and the supposed site of the castle in which Robert Bruce spent his last years and died. North-east of the town in the Kilpatrick Hills is Overtoun Castle, a purely ornamental building with ninety acres of very beautiful countryside, including Overtoun Glen and Spardie Linn, which is open to the public. Entrance is from the Stirling road. Along this road we slowly leave behind the industrialism of the Glasgow district and the beauties of the countryside become more apparent as we near the Burgh of Helensburgh.

Helensburgh

Status: Burgh.
How to Get There: (*By Road*). Bus and coach service from Glasgow with connections from all main centres.
(*By Rail.*) Excellent service from Glasgow with continuation to Oban, Fort William and Mallaig.
Population: 13,327.
Early Closing Day: Wednesday.
Post Office: Colquhoun Square.
Tourist Information Centre: Town Clerk's Office.
Places of Worship: Parish Church, Old and St. Andrew's. Several other denominations are represented.
Parking Places: Excellent and plentiful.
Cinema: La Scala, James Street.
Parks and Open Spaces: West Esplanade, Kidston Park, Hermitage Park, Walker's Rest.
Newspapers: Helensburgh and Gareloch Times (Wednesday), Helensburgh Advertiser (Friday).
Other Amenities: Magnificent walks, fishing, climbing, sailing, golf, bowls, tennis, swimming.

ONE'S FIRST IMPRESSION of Helensburgh is probably, as it is expected to be, of a pleasant seaside town with most of the amenities we have grown to expect. It is, however, the surrounding country and the nearness of Loch Lomond that really make Helensburgh a very well-worth-while stop. Balloch, from where the steamers ply up and down Loch Lomond, is a mere five miles to the east, while the main road continues north-westwards along Gare Loch and Loch Long to Tarbet and Arrochar. Due west of Helensburgh and reached by road through Garelochhead is the Rosneath peninsula of very great beauty. The road runs from Garelochhead around the shores of Gare Loch and Loch Long to finish at the village of Coulport; this is a run worth making, also among the loveliest motor runs is the one along the west bank of Loch Lomond to Tarbet.

Helensburgh is the centre for some delightful short walks and a few long ones; notable among them are the old road to Belmore, across the moors to Loch Lomond and along Glen Douglas from Croggan, on Loch Long, to Loch Lomond.

Proceeding west along the road to Garelochhead note the magnificent pinnacled tower on the Parish Church at Rhu and the glorious scenery along the banks of Gare Loch. Quite a lot of this road and the banks of the loch are occupied by naval and oil installations, especially near Garelochhead. From the height above the village a superb view of Loch Long and Loch Goil can be had, a stop should be made here before proceeding on to the loch-side road to Arrochar through the villages of Arddarroch and Croggan. The scenery along this last stretch is superb.

Arrochar and Tarbet, only a mile and a half apart on the narrow spit of land separating Loch Long from Loch Lomond are very commercialised and thereby lose some of their attraction. Both places are generally busy with day-trippers from the steamers on Loch Lomond.

Westwards from Arrochar is the road to Inveraray and Argyllshire, northwards to Crianlarich and the whole of Northern Scotland, while southwards is that glorious run along the west bank of Loch Lomond to Balloch and Alexandria, both of which places have succumbed to the lure of the thousands of day-trippers and therefore hold little attraction except as the place to board the Loch Lomond steamers in the case of Balloch and to visit the 200 acres of Loch Lomond Park which is very beautiful indeed.

Loch Lomond still remains one of the most beautiful lochs in Scotland. With its many islands and the well-wooded mountains of the Queen Elizabeth Forest to the east it is almost unsurpassed in the sheer beauty of its situation as well as its attraction to the day-tripper. The road along the west bank has been widened and straightened, with the result that a great deal of heavy traffic now uses it.

The Loch Lomond National Nature Reserve, beside including several islands, occupies an area of land on the south-east bank of the Loch south of the Endrick Water. It can be entered on foot only from the Gartocharn–Ross Priory road—this entails only half a mile of walking. For those interested in nature, whether animal or plant, this reserve can afford a day of supreme pleasure. No special permission is required for individuals to visit the five islands of the Nature Reserve but parties should contact the Warden. Full particulars can be obtained from the Nature Conservancy, 9 Hope Terrace, Edinburgh 9, or leaflets describing the Reserve can be obtained from any Information Centre. It should be noted that some parts of the Reserve on the mainland are farmed and permission should be obtained to visit all parts except the Shore Wood.

From Alexandria and Balloch the road heads north-east through Gartocharn, along the southern boundary of the Nature Reserve, across the Endrick Water and into Stirlingshire. Immediately after crossing the bridge note the remarkable picture of Buchanan Castle, now a Golf Club, on the left-hand side. Drymen is in many respects a village of the last century near the banks of the Endrick Water. Nearby is Ducray Castle, typical of the sixteenth century but altered somewhat. Drymen is an extremely pretty place, but offers the visitor modern facilities. From Drymen the main road goes west to Stirling.

From Killearn the nicest road to Falkirk is the B818 over the moors to the north of the Campsie Fells, which contain several delightful walks and much beautiful country on the very edge of the industrial areas; these are best reached from several points along the A891 anywhere between Kilsyth and the A875, which runs south from Killearn to Milngavie. The B818 passes through Fintry, a moorland village close to the Valley of the Endrick Water, or Strathendrick; nearby is the Loup of Fintry, a waterfall over 90 feet in height. The ruin of Sir John de Grahame's castle is about four miles to the east.

Now the B818 passes the tiny Loch Walton and gently downhill past the Carron Valley Reservoir to Carron Bridge. From Killearn this has been a delightful run with high hills around and wooded country in the vicinity of the Reservoir. From Carron Bridge a pleasant little road strikes north past two lochs and through farming country to Stirling, while the B818 continues to industrial Denny and Falkirk.

Falkirk

Status: Burgh.
How to Get There: (*By Rail*). Good service from Edinburgh and Glasgow.
(*By Road.*) Good bus service from Edinburgh, Glasgow and district.
Population: Including immediate surrounding area, 110,000.
Early Closing Day: Wednesday.
Post Office: Vicar Street.
Tourist Information Office: Town Clerk, Municipal Buildings.
Places of Worship: Parish Church, Old Parish Church, Kirk Wynd. There are several Churches of Scotland and most other denominations have places of worship.
Parking Places: Market Square, Callander Riggs, off Callander Road, Garrison Place at Grahamston Station, Vicar Street at Post Office, Howgate off High Street, Williamson Street off Cow Wynd, Municipal Offices, West Bridge Street.
Cinemas: A.B.C., Princes Street, Odeon Theatre, Newmarket Street. Picture House, Bank Street.
Parks and Open Spaces: Callander Park, Victoria Park, Dawson Park, Bellsmeadow, Princes Park, Camelon Public Park, Dollar Park, Easter Carmuirs Park, etc.

Newspaper: Falkirk Herald (Saturday).
Other Amenities: Golf, water-skiing, snow ski-ing, curling, tennis, bowling, putting, angling, concerts, dances,

FALKIRK IS A purley indusfrial town with the status of a Burgh and the reputation of a first-class shopping centre. It is by no means a holiday centre but, if one likes town life, then Falkirk has a lot to offer. Dollar Park and Callander House Gardens are among the best, while water ski-ing can be indulged in at Slamannan on the outer fringes of the Burgh. High Street and the Town Steeple is perhaps the most memorable view of the town itself.

Among the very interesting or beautiful spots in the immediate neighbourhood are the following. Glen Brae, a high spot and completely rural yet overlooking Falkirk; Roughcastle Fort, a Roman fort on the Antonine Wall, access is by footpath from Lime Road, Falkirk; Torphichen Preceptory, headquarters of the Knights of St. John in Scotland; Kinneil, the Palace with some very interesting wall paintings and the little church with an ancient stone crucifix; The Tattie Kirk, off Cow Wynd, an interesting example of post-Reformation architecture in Scotland. There is a small section of country about five miles east of Falkirk known locally as 'up the braes'; it is south-east of Grangemouth, the second port of Scotland and entirely industrial in character, west of the West Lothian border and north of Avonbridge. Surrounded as it is by the mass of industry this is an isolated pocket of real Scottish countryside, of wild and open hillside with just the barest hint of the Highlands; this pocket may be said to extend as far west as Slamannan and is well worth a day's excursion.

The motorist may travel north to Stirling by two routes; the most easterly roughly follows the River Forth past the road-end to the Kincardine Bridge and within a mile into the very ancient, and at one time very important, village of Airth. In 1511 there was a port here and a dockyard for the new fleet of King James IV. A little way from the village is Airth Castle, which is still occupied. The Mercat Cross stands over 17 feet high and is at the north end of the High Street.

A little farther along this road is the picture postcard village of Dunmore, with its very old tower and Tudor mansion. The tower is probably late fifteenth century and has been known as Elphinstone Tower, while the mansion is not likely to be earlier than the early eighteenth century.

The second road is the A9 on which there is little of interest until Bannockburn is reached, some two miles from Stirling centre. This remarkable monument was erected by the National Trust for Scotland. As every schoolboy knows, the English received a sound beating at the hands of the Scots under Robert the Bruce on the 24th of June 1314; although the exact site of the battle is not known it is agreed that the site of this very fine monument is as near as may be. The centre-piece is a statue of King Robert the Bruce on horseback. There is an information centre and the general layout, though modern in concept, is very fine indeed. Two miles beyond this most important piece of Scottish history and the visitor is in the centre of Stirling, county town and one of the most important historical sites in the whole of Scotland.

Stirling

Status: Royal Burgh.
How to Get There: (*By Rail*): Good service from Edinburgh and Glasgow.
(*By Road*.) Good bus service from Edinburgh, Glasgow and district.
Population: 30,050.
Early Closing Day: Wednesday.
Post Office: Murray Place.
Tourist Information Office: Town Clerk's Office, Municipal Buildings, National Trust for Scotland, Borestone, Stirling Tourist Information Centre.
Places of Worship: Parish Church, Church of the Holy Rude. There are a number of Churches of Scotland and most other denominations have places of worship.
Parking Places: Albert Place, Morris Terrace.
Cinema: The Allan Park, Corner of Allan Park and King's Park Road.
Theatres: There are no theatres but local Operatic and Dramatic groups give performances on occasions.
Parks and Open Spaces: Beechwood, Causewayhead, King's Park.
Newspaper: Stirling Observer.
Other Amenities: Bowling, putting, tennis, mini golf, museum, art gallery, children's playgrounds, miniature traffic layout at Beechwood Park, concerts, dances.

ALTHOUGH STIRLING IS not by any means the start of the Highlands yet it is from the ramparts of Stirling Castle that the visitor from the south gets his first view of the massif northwards and westwards; on a clear day the mountains unroll in an endless picture enticing the visitor onwards.

It is impossible in the available space to do justice to such an important centre as Stirling. Let it be said that as far back as history goes, Stirling has been the prize most sought after, for it stands at the head of the Forth estuary and guards the pass to the Highlands. On Castle Hill there are a number of buildings that must be seen. The Castle itself which dates in its present form largely from the fifteenth and sixteenth centuries, contains a wealth of historical treasures.

Argyle House, Mars Wark, two fine old buildings which date respectively from 1630 and 1570. The Church of the Holy Rude, which dates from the fourteenth century or, in parts, earlier. Note the open timber roof, unique in Scotland. The Guildhall or Cowane's Hospital from 1639. The Tolbooth of 1704. The Mercat Cross, of age unknown, with the two cannon. A pleasant and instructive walk is to turn sharp left outside the Guildhall and follow, around three sides, the old Royal Burgh of Stirling. Down in the town itself walk on to the Auld Brig of fourteenth- or fifteenth-century origin and admire the workmanship of those days.

As a modern town Stirling takes a high place, and most visitors, whatever their tastes, will find plenty to enjoy. Just across the Forth, it is necessary to get on to the A91 and, turning off at the first laneway on the right, is Cambuskenneth Abbey. Eight hundred years old, the tower still stands firmly as another example of fine workmanship. In the tower, many years ago, a dug-out canoe was found in a drain or washaway. This has been preserved. There are many other features of interest and beauty in Stirling and the three Information Centres will help the visitor to make his choice.

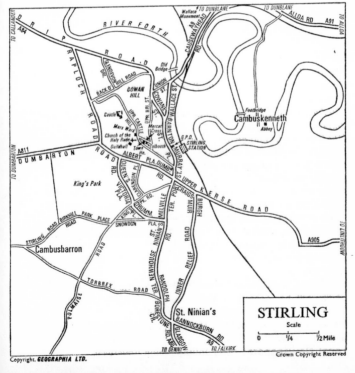

Eight roads radiate from Stirling, three to the south and five to the north and west. We shall now follow the north coast of the Firth of Forth, calling at the Bridge of Allan and the Wallace Monument. This delightful tree-lined little town is a place that invites the visitor to call again; although there is nothing of particular note in the town itself the country to the east and north is superb, that to the west is little less delightful. To the east and north-east are the Ochil Hills and Strathallan over and through which there are some grand routes for walker and motorist alike. Glen Devon in particular attracts many walkers and should attract more. At the north end of the town the water-mill, with the original wheel, should be seen.

The Wallace Monument, reached by turning up the A997 on the return from Bridge of Allan, is one of those particularly fitting monuments which fits the subject, fits the countryside and the hill upon which it stands. The views from this hill are great but from the top of the monument, another 220 feet, they are superb. Taking the A91 and the A907 from the Wallace Monument brings the visitor in less than three miles to the county boundary with Clackmannanshire and a mile or two farther the county town of Alloa.

Alloa

Status: Burgh.
How to Get There: (*By Rail*). From Stirling and Edinburgh–Glasgow.
(*By Air.*) Turnhouse Airport, Edinburgh and Abbotsinch Glasgow thirty miles.
(*By Road.*) Bus and coach services from Stirling, Edinburgh, Glasgow and by connection to all important centres. Less than thirty miles to the Forth Road bridge at North Queensferry.
Population: 13,910.
Early Closing Day: Tuesday.
Post Office: Bedford Place.
Tourist Information Office: Municipal Buildings, Alloa.
Places of Worship: St. Mungo's Parish Church. Several other denominations have places of worship.
Parking Places: Junction Place, off Drysdale Place, Ring Road Car Park.
Cinemas: The Deluxe Cinema, Mill Street, The Pavilion Theatre, Shillinghill, has occasional film showings. Primarily a Bingo Hall.
Theatre: The Alman Players Theatre Club.
Parks and Open Spaces: The West End Park, Ansbrae, Greenfield Grounds, Mar Estate Gardens.
Local Newspapers: Alloa Journal, Alloa Advertiser

Other Amenities: Tennis, bowls, golf and all the attractions of a well-run little county town. In addition the Ochil Hills provide a playground of more than usual beauty.

THIS, THE COUNTY town of the smallest county in the British Isles, has one great claim to fame. George Brown, journalist and newspaper proprietor who emigrated to Canada from Alloa was largely responsible for the founding of the Dominion on 1 July 1867. At one time there was a port here which was used a very little during the last war but is now closed.

The Burgh of Tullibody, close to the western county boundary, has a church of unusual interest, St. Serf's is now a very beautiful ruin with the same type of bellcote as Tillicoultry; against this roofless church is the grave of Sir William Alexander, the founder of Nova Scotia, who emigrated to Canada from Tullibody.

Menstrie Castle, a little north of Tullibody, has been converted into dwelling-houses as part of a new estate. Included is a museum largely of Nova Scotia and the Abercrombie family.

Some three miles north of Tullibody is the little industrial Burgh of Alva. It is a friendly town of some 4,000 inhabitants with the bulk of its people engaged in the woollen mills as well as many other industrial concerns. In the seventeenth century silver was mined locally but was never a profitable venture. The Silver Glen, which winds into the Ochil Hills a little east of the town, is a reminder of those days. The name Alva is Celtic in origin and means 'the rock plain'. St. Serf was a visitor here and in 1600 a church was built and dedicated to him. Many are the delightful walks that can be started at Alva and continued into the Ochil Hills.

About three miles east of Alva is the quite small holiday resort and Burgh of Tillicoultry in the Devon Valley, at the very feet of the Ochil Hills. It is the truly beautiful combination of the Devon River with the Ochils and the many wild glens that wind and twist into these 2,000-foot hills that gives this little county of Clackmannanshire its great attractiveness. It may with truth be said that the Devon Valley, the Ochils and the many glens, in particular the Alva Glen, the Tillicoultry Glen, the Gartmorn Loch and the Daiglen Burn make this tiny corner of Scotland one of the beauty-spots. For those who like rougher expeditions there are many peaks to be climbed and the hill walks are endless in their variety.

A little farther west and right on the county boundary with Perthshire is the little town with the famous Academy. This was founded in 1818 on the bequest of £100,000 by a local man, McNab, who, starting as a cattle-herd, went to sea and became a great shipowner. The Burgh of Dollar is the name of this little place and it is supposed to be a misspelling of Dolour. Several other names in the immediate district will raise questions; between the Glen of Care and the Burn of Sorrow high on a hillock stands Castle Gloom, now generally referred to as Castle Campbell and in charge of the National Trust for Scotland. This is a quite short walk and one of the most beautiful in a corner of Northern Scotland where beautiful walks abound.

Rather less than three miles south-east of Alloa is the former county town of Clackmannanshire; Clackmannan is an extremely nice little town with one of the most interesting and oldest relics in the county. The Mannan Stone was sacred to the pre-Christian Deity and stood, no doubt as an object of worship, at the foot of Lookabootye Brae. It has now been set up in the town centre with a seventeenth-century cross and a Tolbooth dated 1592.

Less than a mile and a half from Clackmannan the motorist crosses the county boundary into the Kingdom of Fife and one of the most interesting counties in Northern Scotland. Tulliallan Castle, seen immediately before entering Kincardine, is a Police College and of no interest to the average holidaymaker. Kincardine is a purely industrial and dormitory town. The Mercat Cross and a few examples of Scottish architecture provide the greatest interest. It is a good shopping centre and a useful stop for the motorist going farther afield. A long while ago Kincardine was a seaport and shipbuilding centre and is today the northern end of the Kincardine Road Bridge which, until the opening of the Forth Road Bridge, was the only bridge lower than Stirling.

Following the A985, the coast road eastwards from Kincardine, the visitor very soon arrives at Culross, which is largely under the auspices of the National Trust for Scotland and one of the few completely unspoiled and almost entirely seventeenth-century towns in Northern Scotland. As a Royal Burgh Culross has a history going back into the dim and distant past. St. Mungo's Chapel, or the remains thereof, represent the first beginnings, for here St. Mungo was born and was educated by St. Serf and later in life founded the Cathedral of Glasgow. This chapel was built and dedicated to him in 1503.

On the eastern side of Culross is Dunimarle Castle, associated sometimes with the murder of Lady Macduff and her children by order of Macbeth. The name Dunimarle is Gaelic for 'the Castle on the Cliff', it has a quite fantastic appearance and is open to the public at certain times; it includes many fine treasures.

Culross Abbey was founded in 1217 by Malcolm Earl of Fife, and at least one of the original walls remains. It is now the Parish Kirk in its rebuilt condition. From the churchyard some fine views of the Forth can be had. The remains of the Monastery are in the charge of the Dept. of Environment. Culross Abbey House dates from 1610. From the Abbey Kirk Street runs steeply downhill to the 'new' town of the sixteenth and seventeenth centuries. On the left are the

Coachman's Cottage and Snuff Cottage, both of 1673. Farther down is Butcher's House, 1664. All these are well worth inspection. The Mercat Cross is the centre of the Burgh and was erected in 1588. From the Cross there are a number of streets radiating all with many houses and buildings owned by the National Trust for Scotland and all of the sixteenth and seventeenth centuries. There are many, many more places in Culross that the visitor will wish to see—one that should not be missed is the Palace of Culross, built in 1597–1611.

Dunfermline

Status: City and Royal Burgh.
How to Get There: (*By rail*). From Edinburgh and Glasgow. (*By Road.*) Bus and coach services direct or by connection to all important centres.
Population: 51,798.
Early Closing Day: Wednesday.
Post Office: Corner of Queen Anne Street and Pilmuir Street.
Tourist Information Centre: Town Clerk's Office.
Places of Worship: Parish Church, Dunfermline Abbey. Many other denominations have places of worship.
Parking Places: North end of Chalmers Street and Bruce Street, Abbot Street, Park Avenue.
Cinemas: Cinema, East Port, Regal, High Street, Palace Cinema, Rosyth.
Parks and Open Spaces: Pittencrieff Park.
Local Newspaper: The Dunfermline Press (Fridays).
Other Amenities: Swimming, athletics, angling, hockey, putting, golf. A rich cultural programme.

THE ANCIENT CAPITAL of Scotland and burial place of many of her Kings, Dunfermline is a worthy city with both old and modern blending perfectly. As with so many of the most important towns it is impossible to describe and list all the places the visitor will want to see; the main points of interest will be mentioned.

The history of Dunfermline goes back to Pictish days when they had a fort at Pittencrieff. The remains of this fort can still be seen in Pittencrieff Park, which was given to the city by that great citizen, Andrew Carnegie, who as a lad emigrated with his parents to America to become one of its richest industrialists. Among the many gifts to Scotland was a trust fund for Dunfermline which assures the city of a yearly income which has been used for the welfare of the people.

Malcolm Canmore was possibly the first king to reside at Dunfermline, this was in the eleventh century. The Abbey was founded in 1070 by Margaret, wife of Malcolm Canmore. Part of this ancient edifice, rebuilt, is now the Parish Kirk. The remains of the Monastery date from the twelfth century while the Palace, in its oldest parts, is probably a good deal more ancient. Many old houses are to be seen and admired by the visitor with a keen and discerning eye.

As a modern town and shopping centre Dunfermline will be hard to beat; it is a good centre from which to explore the ancient Kingdom of Fife and the whole coastline of the Firth of Forth and the North Sea, which is very beautiful and extensive.

About two to three miles south-west of Dunfermline on the Forth shore-line are two interesting villages; in Charlestown is a model eighteenth century village and at the foot of the cliffs are some lime-kilns cut out of the solid rock which are very spectacular. The village of Limekilns, one mile east of Charlestown, is mentioned in Stevenson's *Kidnapped*. It also boasts a very ancient stone-vaulted building known as King's Cellars. Since Limekilns was once a port it seems probable that imports of wine, etc., were stored here for Dunfermline Palace.

Farther east again is Rosyth Dockyard and Inverkeithing, which is a great deal more ancient than might be supposed; the first charter was granted in 1165. There are a few interesting buildings of great age, the Parish Church of St. Peter, twelfth century, the Hospitium of Greyfriars Monastery, fourteenth century, and in addition there are a number of sixteenth-century houses still occupied. Rosyth Castle can be seen by arrangement with the Dept. of Environment. North Queensferry named after Malcolm Canmore's Queen, had a ferry service which operated for 800 years until the Forth Road Bridge was opened. It was at North Queensferry that the builders of the Forth Railway Bridge had their northern base. The construction started in 1890 and 5,000 men were employed. Of these, 57 were killed and 500 injured. The total cost was just over three million pounds. Eastwards the road follows the Firth to Aberdour, while the M90 motorway strikes northwards for the Tay Bridge, Dundee and Aberdeen.

Aberdour is reputed to be one of the most popular resorts on the Fife coast; there is a fine beach of silver sand with a large park and café as well as excellent car-parking arrangements. Whichever way you look from the hilltop on the short walk to St. Bridgets the view is superb; landwards are the Ochil Hills, eastwards the widening Firth of Forth while southwards the Lammermuirs and the Pentlands form a fine backcloth to the immediate prospect of the narrowing Firth and Edinburgh.

Within, or very close to, Aberdour there are a number of interesting features to be seen. The Castle of Aberdour, built in the thirteenth or very early fourteenth century, stands high on a bank close to the Dour Burn. Fairly early in its life it came into the hands of the Douglas family who still retain ownership. It is in the charge of the Dept. of Environment and is open to the public. The lovely little church of St.

Fillan's which stands alongside the road to the Silver Sands is in all probability very early twelfth century and is regarded as one of the gems of Scottish church architecture. The bellcote and cracked bell came from the twelfth- or thirteenth-century chapel at St. Bridgets. This is another lovely old church under the Dept. of Environment and open to the public.

South of Aberdour and about two miles from the tiny harbour is the Island of Inchcolm, with the Abbey and Priory of St. Colms. In 1123 the island was occupied by a hermit, and in the same year King Alexander I founded the Monastery of which a great deal, including the original cell of the hermit, can be seen today. Boats sail from Aberdour but much depends on the conditions of weather and tide.

The visitor bent on seeing the best of Fifeshire will keep to the coast road to Burntisland which is a pleasant mixture of holiday facilities and shipbuilding. Tradition has it that the Romans established a port here and a fort on Dunearn Hill; if so, then Burntisland has 2,000 years of seafaring history. Today it is a Royal Burgh and a prosperous and very pleasant holiday resort with an outdoor swimming-pool that was originally constructed to Olympic standards. At one time Burntisland belonged to the Monks of Dunfermline who built a castle at Rossend and the little Kirk at Kirkston.

The coast road continues very close to the coast to Pettycur and Kinghorn, with the hills, heavily wooded, rising nearly straight up on the left. Pettycur is a tiny place with a caravan camp while Kinghorn stands near the point of Kinghorn Ness, that broad buttress of land which projects into the Firth of Forth opposite Edinburgh.

The Burgh of Kinghorn has for many centuries been a popular holiday resort, in the past for kings and nobility of Scotland, today with the ordinary man. It is also a popular dormitory for Kirkcaldy. Two miles out in the Firth is the island of Inchkeith, with a lighthouse. For many centuries this island, lying midway between Kirkcaldy and Edinburgh, has been fortified and it strongly protected the entrance to the River Forth. As a shipbuilding centre and spinning town Kinghorn was once a great deal more important industrially.

Kirkcaldy

Status: Royal Burgh.
How to Get There: (*By Rail*). On the main line north from Edinburgh to Aberdeen.
(*By Air.*) Turnhouse Airport, Edinburgh, is less than twenty-five miles.
(*By Road.*) Bus and coach services from Edinburgh and by connection with all important centres. Forth Road Bridge no more than fifteen miles.
Population: 52,125.
Early Closing Day: Wednesday.

Post Office: Hunter Street.
Tourist Information Centre: Fife Tourist Association,
Esplanade (April–September).
Places of Worship: Parish Church, Kirkcaldy Old Parish Church.
A number of other denominations have places of worship.
Parking Places: Esplanade.
Cinemas: Odeon, High Street, A.B.C. Cinema, High Street, Rio
Cinema, St. Clair Street.
Parks and Open Spaces: Ravenscraig Park, Beveridge Park,
Dunnikier Park.
Local Newspaper: Fife Free Press (Friday).
Other Amenities: Water ski-ing on Gelly Loch, motor-cycle racing,
bathing, ten-pin bowling alley, dancing, greyhound racing, golf,
ice rink, curling, fishing.

KNOWN AS THE 'Lang Toon O'Fife', Kirkcaldy is a Royal Burgh and a
most important industrial town as well as a popular holiday resort.
Right through the ages Kirkcaldy has played a most important part in
the affairs of the ancient Kingdom of Fife. In wrought iron on the top
of the Town House is the Patron Saint of the Burgh, St. Bryce. Many
people of world-wide fame were born in Kirkcaldy, including that
great Australian explorer, John MacDougall Stuart, who also founded
The Scotsman. The present Burgh is composed of the three ancient
communities of Linktown, Pathhead and Gallatown, and is established
around the Bay of Kirkcaldy and stretches as far north as Ravenscraig
and Dysart.

During the last century it was linoleum that brought about the
greatest prosperity, and to a large extent still contributes more than
its share to the diversified industrial life of the Burgh. The harbour
was once far more important than it is today although there is a
deepwater dock and much shipping uses the port.

From the holidaymaker's point of view the promenade and the long
stretch of foreshore including the very beautiful woodland-backed
sands at Ravenscraig are perhaps the chief attraction. The several very
delightful parks add their quota to the generally pleasant holiday
atmosphere of Kirkcaldy. Among the older buildings are some houses
in Sailor's Walk near the Harbour, and Ravenscraig Castle, of 1460,
which is under the auspices of the Dept. of Environment and is open
to the public. The tower of the Parish Church, with lancet windows of
the thirteenth or fourteenth century, has been in use for close on
seven hundred years. As a shopping centre Kirkcaldy has a very high
reputation indeed. On the first of January every year an old custom
is kept alive by a game of kyles. This is the rolling of an iron ball
towards a hole, and if it enters the hole, it is kyled. Cannon balls
were used in the old days.

Continuing northwards along the coast road the visitor will sense

Duntugh Castle, Skye

Glamis Castle

St. Andrews Royal and Ancient

Skiing, Aviemore

that the industrial areas have been virtually left behind, and ahead lies the best of Fifeshire and the best of the coastline. The next two small places are West and East Wemyss, and the coal-town of Wemyss. These are purely residential areas which skirt the estate and Castle of Wemyss where there are caves with Bronze Age drawings of hunting scenes and Pagan Gods. A little past East Wemyss on the seaward side of the road is the ruin of Macduff Castle. At Buckhaven the road draws close to the shore again.

Methil is the seaport for both Buckhaven and Leven. Of the latter place it can be said that nearly everything the modern holidaymaker asks for is supplied; sands, parks, caravan sites, good shops and a pleasant situation. In Scoonie churchyard are the remains of the well-known Scoonie Church of the eleventh century. The Scoonie Stone was discovered here with animal carvings and an inscription in the Ogham tongue of more than a thousand years ago. It was presented to the Antiquarian Museum.

Eastwards from Leven comes the great sweep of Largo Bay and right in the middle are the three-villages-in-one of Upper Largo, Lundin Links and Lower Largo. Just outside Lundin Links there is a set of Standing Stones which may indicate a connection with the Druids. Upper Largo is a nice rural village with a quite impressive kirk while Lower Largo is famous for its statue of 'Robinson Crusoe'— Alexander Selkirk, whose adventures inspired the story was in Lower Largo when that village was a very busy fishing port. The beach has a small spread of sand and much rock but the atmosphere is the all-important factor.

Next to the east and right on the eastern point of Largo Bay, which is, overall, one long crescent of clean sand dominated by the height of Largo Law which nearly reaches a thousand feet, are the two villages of Elie and Earlsferry, now included in the Royal Burgh of Earlsferry but known as 'The Elie'. Here there is a first-rate fishing harbour and all those almost undefined things that go to make a wholly delightful seaside village. In 1589 Earlsferry was described as 'old beyond the memory of man'; both these villages are no doubt very ancient and retain their attractions to a marked degree.

From here on the coast loses its low aspect and becomes largely rock-girt. The burgh of St. Monance is the next little place and remembered for its remarkable little church of over six hundred years of age. The Burgh of St. Monance can only be remembered as a village and a very lovely one. It sits on the east side of the Inverie Burn while the church is high up on the west side and in view from land or sea. In A.D. 832 St. Monance, in the company of another Irish priest named Adrian, is reputed to have been the first to preach the gospel in the island of May some ten miles offshore from St. Monance; he was slain by Danish invaders in A.D. 875 and his shrine is reputed to be close to the church, which was founded in A.D. 1265–7.

Like most Scottish churches this one suffered from fire and sword and was finally damaged by a mine during the last war. However, it has been renovated and is one that should not be missed by anyone with a liking for church architecture of the past.

Quite close to the kirk are the ruins of Newark Castle, on a headland nearly surrounded by stark, pointed rocks and in a very prominent position. The little Burgh has been famous for the quality of its boat-building for centuries, one family having been building here for two hundred years. This is a village with the beauty of the old, narrow streets, red tiled roofs and crow-stepped gables, plus the atmosphere that grows with an old fishing village. A few of the more modern amenities have been introduced but not to the extent that would spoil the age-old attractions.

Three miles farther up the coast is the Royal Burgh of Pittenweem whose chief industry is, and always has been, fishing. A modern fish market on the quay is always a source of interest. This quite sizeable little town is full of old and picturesque houses, and many have been preserved by the National Trust for Scotland and the East Neuk of Fife Preservation Society. The Parish Kirk, with a balustrade around the tower top and the old prison at the foot, is particularly well worth a visit; very close to the kirk is the Mercat Cross and the Tolbooth.

The Royal Burgh of Kilrenny, Anstruther, Anstruther Easter and Anstruther Wester is the longest name in Scotland and the next little place on the coast; fortunately it is now known simply as Anstruther. Until sometime in the 1940s this was the capital of the winter herring

Wallace Monument

fishing in Scotland. The herring have since deserted their once usual grounds in the Firth of Forth. Half a dozen boats still fish distant grounds and return occasionally. Other industries, chiefly the tourist trade, have replaced fishing. Nearby at Cellardyke a holiday camp has been established on an old R.A.F. station. As in Pittenweem there are many old houses, narrow steets and the atmosphere that successfully combines ancient and modern into an attractive whole. Anstruther is the port for the Isle of May, but much depends on weather and tide. The island is largely rockbound, has a lighthouse and is a Sea Bird Sanctuary. The National Trust for Scotland has taken over St. Ayles' Chapel and converted part of this old building into a fishing museum; also in their hands is Buckie House in West Anstruther, decorated inside and out with sea-shells. The Mercat Cross and Tolbooth are two interesting features.

After passing the village of Kilrenny and following fairly closely the coast, Crail is reached and the nearest point to Fife Ness. It is a Royal Burgh, a fishing port and a popular holiday resort. This lovely place is in many respects a replica of the other ancient fishing ports along this latter stretch which is largely rock-bound and the more picturesque for that. Here again the National Trust for Scotland has taken over many old houses and buildings. The Town Hall, or Town House, the ancient Church of St. Mary's and the Mercat Cross, as well as many ordinary houses, are well worth inspection by those with a liking for the craftsmanship of long ago. Close to the golf-links at Balcomie is a cottage that marks all that remains of the Royal Burgh of Fifeness. The walk to the point of Fife Ness is perhaps the most delightful part of a visit to Crail; from this high outstanding point of rock which divides the Firth of Tay from the Firth of Forth there are some wonderful views; here also the bird watcher will find absorbing interest. Balcomie Castle is part of the farm a mile before the Ness. From the Ness one can see the Inchcape or Bell Rock upon which the Abbott fastened a bell to warn shipping. Ralph the Rover removed it so that ships could more easily become wrecked and looted; within a year he was caught in a storm and wrecked on the Bell Rock; today there is a lighthouse.

Between Crail and St. Andrews there are two places on the coast road, Kingbarns, with a striking church spire, and Boarhills, a name which commemorates the hunting of wild boar in days long gone by. About six miles north of Boarhills is the famous golfing city of St. Andrews. The best entrance by far is by the direct road from Anstruther, through the village of Dunino with its 800-year-old kirk under the Dept. of Environment, for, by this route, one mile before entering St. Andrews the road tops St. Nicholas Brae from which point the view of the 'Old Grey City' is truly superb. Around the coast of Fife the villages most worth a visit—and they are supremely beautiful —are Culross, Elie, St. Monance, Pittenweem, Anstruther and Crail.

St. Andrews

Status: Royal Burgh, University Town.

How to Get There: By Rail. From Leuchars Junction which is on the main Edinburgh–Dundee–Aberdeen line.

(*By Road.*) St. Andrews has an excellent local bus service with bus and coach connections, or through services, to Dundee, Perth and Glasgow. The bus station is off City Road.

Population: The Burgh, 12,000.

Early Closing Day: Thursday.

Post Office: South Street.

Tourist Information Centre: South Street.

Places of Worship: Parish Church, the Town Kirk of Holy Trinity. Many other denominations have places of worship.

Parking Places: Numerous and well marked. The West Sands can take several thousand.

Cinemas: Cinema House, North Street, The New Picture House, North Street.

Theatre: The Byre Theatre, Abbey Street.

Parks and Open Spaces: Kinburn Park, Cockshaugh Park, Craigtoun Park.

Local Newspaper: The St. Andrews Citizen (Friday).

Other Amenities: Golf, swimming, tennis, bowls, boating, fishing.

FOR OLDER PEOPLE St. Andrews must be the most interesting town, apart from Edinburgh, in Scotland. For younger folks most of the modern seaside amenities are to hand; so that all in all St. Andrews can claim to be in the forefront of holiday resorts.

As long ago as the middle 700s there was a religious house here of which the ruins of the Cathedral probably cover some remains. The Burgh of St. Andrews and the Cathedral began to take shape in the early part of the twelfth century and from that time onwards grew in importance. At the consecration of the Cathedral in 1318 this was the largest church in Scotland and the ruins today are among the finest.

There is so much to be seen in St. Andrews that a list of the most important spots seems to be the only way to enlighten the visitor.

The Cathedral and Priory were founded in 1160; the Priory was one of the most important religious foundations of its time. The attached Museum contains many old and interesting relics.

St. Rule's Church was founded in the very early thirteenth century and the square tower is among the most remarkable of its kind in Scotland. Holy Trinity Church, known as the Town Kirk, was founded in 1410 and restored in the early years of this century. It is among the finest parish churches in Scotland.

St. Leonard's Chapel, founded in the first few years of the

sixteenth century and restored some years ago ; it is still in use as the Chapel of St. Leonard's College.

The West Port was built in 1589, as the principal entrance to the old city, and today is the finest example of a Burgh gate in Scotland.

The Pends was originally a vaulted gatehouse and the main entrance to the Priory Precinct and dates from the late fourteenth century ; the Precinct Wall dates from 200 years later.

St. Salvator's College and part of the many scattered buildings of the University of St. Andrews. This was founded in 1450 and the present building contains the original Tower and Collegiate Church.

The Castle was built in 1200 as a fortress but became the residence of the Bishops. The bottle dungeon should definitely be seen.

The Harbour is one of the most picturesque scenes of St. Andrews. Its age is unknown but the pier was rebuilt in the seventeenth century with stone from the Cathedral and Castle.

Of the above list the following are in the charge of the Dept. of Environment : the Cathedral and Priory, St. Rule's Church, the West Port, the Pends and Precinct Wall, the Castle. In addition the Dept. of Environment have charge of St. Mary's Kirk and St. Rule's Museum. Both these are well worth a visit.

Both east and west of St. Andrews there are glorious sandy beaches while between the giant Rock of Dhu Craig and the Harbour there is a small boating beach, many rocky outcrops, the Castle on its high promontory and beneath its walls another bathing beach and St. Rule's Cave. Eastwards from the East Sands are the Kinkell Braes which embrace a cliff-top path with some glorious views and many tiny little-used coves where peace and quiet can be enjoyed. Three geological freaks are to be seen on this route, the Maiden Rock and the Rock and Spindle. Altogether the St. Andrews coastline is more than attractive.

Now the fishing industry has largely died St. Andrews has become a great centre for sailing for which the old Harbour seems to be ideal. There are several parks of which Craigtoun deserves special mention. Three miles west of St. Andrews, the grounds are owned by Fifeshire County Council and are particularly beautiful. Its many acres of grassland, its rose garden, Cypress Walk and the Dutch Village on an island in the lake make this a quite exceptional park, especially for children.

In cultural activities, as one would suppose, St. Andrews is a busy place, both in winter and summer, and dancing takes a big place in the list of events. Naturally golf has pride of place in this, the home of the game. There are four courses and they are open to all to play whether members of the Royal and Ancient Golf Club or not. During the busy season one has to ballot for starting time. The Old Course is generally agreed by the most famous golfers to be the finest course in the world. Golf was played here as long ago as 1547. Both monks

and kings played and helped to establish the great tradition and
reputation of the Royal and Ancient. Apart from all these things and
many others St. Andrews is a charming town and a very good
shopping centre.

Inland from St. Andrews the land rises to a range of low hills. The
soil is not rich and grazing is the chief farming occupation.

Ceres is a delightful village with the sculpture of a jovial and
smiling Provost to greet the visitor at the road end. Here the Fife
Folk Museum is a must, as is the Scotstarvit Tower on the hill close
to the National Trust for Scotland property of Scotstarvit House,
which has been taken over by the Marie Curie Memorial Foundation;
it is open to the public at certain times. The Tower is in charge of the
Dept. of Environment, and both are well worth a visit, for the views
from the Tower and the furniture, pictures, etc., in the House. Three
to four miles north of Ceres is Cupar, the County Town of Fifeshire.

Cupar

Status: Royal Burgh.
How to Get There: (*By Rail*). Main-line service from King's Cross
on the Dundee–Aberdeen line.
(*By Road.*) Excellent bus and coach service from Dundee, Stirling
and surrounding area with connections to all important centres.
Population: 6,013 approx.
Early Closing Day: Thursday.
Post Office: Crossgate.
Tourist Information Centre: Town Clerks Office and the Fife
Tourist Association, High Street, Leven.
Places of Worship: Cupar Old Church. One or two other
denominations have places of worship.
Parking Places: Fluthers car park, Burnside, temporary car park at
Bonnygate.
Cinema: La Scala, Westport.
Parks and Open Spaces: The Cart Haugh, Hood Park, Nicolson
Park, The Duffus Park.
Local Newspapers: Fife Herald (weekly), Fife News (weekly),
Evening Telegraph and Post (daily), Dundee Courier and Advertiser
(daily), People's Journal (weekly).
Other Amenities: Apart from the several beautiful parks and
surrounding countryside, cricket, tennis, bowls and most sports are
represented.

CUPAR HAS A particularly friendly atmosphere but no buildings of
great age. As a Royal Burgh Cupar has a history going back as far as

the twelfth century and in all probability long before. The Thanes of Fife had their castle overlooking the eastern approaches to the town. There was a monastery here but as with the castle Cupar prefers to look to the present and the future rather than the past; old rubs shoulders with new, narrow streets with broad thoroughfares, creating a very pleasant, but not nostalgic, scene. Cupar is based, industrially, on agriculture and is the centre of a very wide agricultural area. One of the most impressive monuments in the town is the War Memorial whilst the Mercat Cross and the Parish Kirk have features of great interest.

Three miles north-west of Cupar is The Mount, topped by a Doric column one hundred feet in height. From its summit one can see right across the Tay to the massive hills of the Highlands on a clear day. Many are the glens and ridges around Cupar that should attract the less adventurous for their beauty and quiet rural atmosphere. Westwards from the Burgh the country is pleasantly agricultural, not too hilly and not too flat, with a number of tidy villages and the River Eden, which rises a few miles east of the border with Kinross. At the foot of the Lomond Hills, where the A912 and the A983 meet, is Falkland Palace, a National Trust for Scotland property. This is one of the most important National Trust properties to be seen. It was completed in 1542 and has royal connections going back to the thirteenth century. There is an Information Centre on the site. Westwards from Cupar the Valley of the Eden, which is closely followed by the A91, leads to Guardbridge not far north of St. Andrews.

Although today Guardbridge is an industrial village it was once little more than the guard-house for the bridge across the Eden; this fourteenth-century bridge can be seen today alongside the new one. It was also the port for St. Andrews and Cupar. Near the village of Strathkinness, which is on a narrow side-road south of Guardbridge, is a magnificent view from the crest of the hill of a great deal of the east coast and northwards to the Cairngorms.

Two miles north of Guardbridge is the R.A.F. village of Leuchars, which stages a Battle of Britain Air Display every year. The chief attraction is the Parish Church, which has an apse and chancel that is reputed to be the best of this class of Norman work in Scotland; it is thirteenth century. Leuchars is the largest R.A.F. station in Scotland. North-east of Leuchars, towards the coast and the mouth of the Tay, there is a large area without roads that has been taken over by the Forestry Commission, part of which is a bird sanctuary. An interesting old industry that flourished for a very long period was the cultivation of mussels for fish bait all along the east coast of Fifeshire.

Tayport is in the Parish of Ferry-Port-on-Craig and for many hundreds of years until 1939 was the embarkation point for the ferry crossing to Broughty Ferry. Today this very old place is almost entirely industrial but shows signs of becoming a holiday resort. From the hill west of Tayport a remarkable view of the River Tay and the Tay Bridges can be had as well as the city of Dundee; on a clear evening this should be a truly magnificent scene. The next place along the Tay is Newport-on-Tay. Industrial and busy best describes this town which sits almost under the Tay road-bridge. Wormit, at the southern end of the Tay railway-bridge, claims to be the first village in Scotland to have electric light, which was generated from a windmill. This was also the scene of the fearful railway disaster of 1879 when the nearly new railway-bridge collapsed and a train with a hundred passengers plunged into the river with a complete loss of life.

Close by is the village of Gauldry near which are the remains of Balmerino Abbey, under the auspices of the National Trust for Scotland.

Lindores Loch, on the road from Cupar to Newburgh, is a very pleasant little spot with nothing special to recommend it—the riverside road is by far the most attractive. Lindores Abbey, on the riverside road immediately before entering Newburgh, was one of the great religious houses of Fife during the Middle Ages, it was founded in 1178. The remains are still worth viewing.

Newburgh, on the Perthshire border, is a purely industrial Burgh although with a particularly pleasant and welcoming atmosphere. The Cross of Mugdrum stands on the riverside close to the town and is 13 feet in height and is supposed to have been carved with an attractive design 1,300 years ago. Less than twelve miles north-west is Perth.

Kinross

Status: Burgh.
How to Get There: (*By Road*). Excellent bus service from Edinburgh with connections to all important centres.
Population: 3,000.
Early Closing Day: Thursday.
Post Office: High Street.
Tourist Information Office: Green Hotel.
Places of Worship: Parish Church, West Church. A few other denominations have places of worship.
Parking Places: Car-parking is not a serious problem and no special car-parks are set aside; there is ample room.
Cinema: The County Cinema, High Street.
Parks and Open Spaces: Kirkgate, adjoining Loch Leven, with putting-green, children's amusements, etc.

Other Amenities: Angling, curling, skating, golf, bowls, walking.

ALTHOUGH KINROSS-SHIRE was a long while ago a part of the
Kingdom of Fife it is now a county and the second smallest in
Scotland; it is in a particularly fortunate situation being almost
surrounded by hills so that the climate is equable, the land both rich
and varied while the countryside is delightfully attractive. In the
centre of this tiny county is the northern end of Loch Leven and
the County Town of Kinross; indeed, there is only one other
town, Milnathorpe.

Kinross is a very nice little town indeed but it is as a centre from
which to explore the Shire that Kinross offers most attraction. Loch
Leven is the jewel which mirrors the surrounding hills; the Lomond
Hills to the east which rise to little more than 1,000 feet; southwards
are the Cleish Hills. No higher than the Lomonds they are green and
lovely while keeping at bay the coalfields of southern Fifeshire. To
the west and north are the long line of the rugged Ochils which
tower to well over 2,000 feet and hide within their Glens and tops
some of the most glorious country south of the Highlands. Kinross-shire
has been called the 'Sleepy Hollow of Scotland'.

Loch Leven has seen most of the history connected with Kinross
and on it are several islands which have contributed to this history.
The name Kinross is derived from the Gaelic, a promontory, which
refers to the position of Kinross town in relation to Loch Leven, which
is one of the few remaining of the many lochs that were in Fife and
Kinross in the seventeenth century. On its placid waters, on a really
still day, the outline of Bishops Hill and the further Lomonds can be
clearly seen mirrored in distinct outline, or, from the right position,
the more rugged Ochils show even more clearly.

On one of the islands are the ruins of Leven Castle in which Mary
Queen of Scots was imprisoned in 1567; the surrounding wall, the
central keep and one tower remain and are in the charge of the
Dept. of Environment; its exact age is unknown but is likely to be
thirteenth or fourteenth century. Another island, to the south-east of
Leven Castle, was the home of St. Serf, and the rather fragmentary
remains of the Priory can still be viewed; it was founded in the
eighth century by the Culdee Sect, the strongest survival of the
Celtic beliefs. Boats will take visitors to both these islands.

Loch Leven trout are noted among fishermen as some of the finest
and the sport is still popular; competitions are held at intervals.
The banks of the Loch, adjacent to the town, are a popular public
park and at the far end is the Watchtower at the entrance to an old
graveyard. These watchtowers were used to house watchmen in the
days when medical science was badly in need of human bodies to
experiment on; these were frequently unearthed from the grave and
taken to Edinburgh for a suitable reward.

Milnathorpe, one mile north of Kinross, is a clean and welcoming town with golf, tennis and other amenities for the visitor. Close by are the remains of Burleigh Castle, the ancient seat of the Balfours of Burleigh. In a field close by are the Standing Stones of Orwell, which are thought to represent some pre-Christian era. Both are in the hands of the Dept. of Environment.

Milnathorpe is close to the foothills of the Ochils and makes an excellent centre from which to explore the glens and burns of these rugged and roughed-topped hills.

In the country east of Kinross, towards the Lomond Hills, there are many lovely villages and a countryside as beautiful as any with green fields and woods rising to the outline of the Lomonds. Portmoak Parish contains a very ancient tower that was built in the thirteenth century by the Arnots, who were continuously living there or connected with their old home until the nineteenth century. It measures 31 feet by 24 feet with walls 6 feet thick, and stands among the woods and fields at the foot of West Lomond, a hill with a particularly attractive appearance. Today there is a considerable amount of gliding done among the hot air currents generated by these hills. Much of this country was famous for its health-giving springs and wells.

South-west of Kinross are the Cleish Hills, green, gentle and very beautiful. The Parish Church is said to stand on the site of an ancient ecclesiastical foundation; in the churchyard is a stone commemorating William Michie, a schoolmaster, and the epitaph was written by Robert Burns:

> *Here lie Willie Michie's banes,*
> *O Satan ! when ye tak' him*
> *Gie him the schoolin' o' your weans,*
> *For clever deils he'll mak'em !*

The road over the Cleish Hills via Crook of Devon gives a quite remarkable view of what appears to be the whole of Kinross-shire.

The north-west of the county is perhaps the finest from the scenic viewpoint. Here the lovely Devon River which rises in the heart of the Ochils flows through pastoral areas, makes a sharp turn at the Crook of Devon and a deep rumbling noise at Rumbling Bridge before it leaves the county of Kinross. Rumbling Bridge is a centre with an hotel ; there are waterfalls and rills that compare favourably with any. The 120-foot gorge is spanned by a bridge and the remains of the early eighteenth-century bridge can be seen below. The Crook of Devon is another delightful village with the nearby remains of Tulliebole Castle.

Section 3. The Highlands south of the Great Glen

Dunblane

Status: City and Burgh.
How to Get There: (*By Rail*). Excellent services from London, Edinburgh and Glasgow.
(*By Road.*) First-class bus and coach services from Stirling and Perth with connections to all important centres.
Population: 5,222.
Early Closing Day: Wednesday.
Post Office: Stirling Road.
Tourist Information Centre: Town Clerk's Office.
Places of Worship: Parish Church, Dunblane Cathedral. Several other denominations have places of worship.
Parking Places. Millrow, Cathedral Square, Haining, Station Road.
Parks and Open Spaces: The Laighills, Ochlochy Park.
Newspaper: The Stirling Observer (Wednesday and Friday).
Other Amenities: Golf, tennis, bowls, fishing, swimming at the Dunblane Hotel Hydro which is open to non-residents.

TRAVELLING NORTHWARDS FROM Stirling, along the A9 which follows the Allan Water through the narrow gap known as Strathallan, it is interesting to remember that this road, the old Great North Road, is the most historic road in Scotland. The Romans came this way, and right through history this has been the only route to the Highlands and the green straths and carses of the east coast. Between the Ochil Hills and the far-flung southern outposts of the Grampians the Allan and the road thread their way amidst beautiful scenery that is somewhat spoiled by the constant flow of traffic.

The first place of note is Dunblane, as cosy a little Cathedral City and Burgh as it would be possible to find. Situated at the extreme southern boundary of Perthshire, Dunblane occupies a delightful position on the banks of the Allan Water among trees and gardens. Although not a Highland town Dunblane is the point from which two roads reach out into the Highland foothills, and has, for over a thousand years, been an important religious centre. The Church which preceded the present Cathedral was founded by St. Blane in the early seventh century. He was a member of the Culdee Sect, the survivors of the ancient Celtic Church. During the twelfth century Dunblane became a Bishopric and the Cathedral quickly followed. The lower portion of the tower is all that is left of this, the first Cathedral. Among the many beautiful and historic features there are two that stand right out: the carving of the fifteenth-century choir-stalls, unique in Scotland, and the decoration of the west window in which the sculptor used only forest leaves instead of the more formal dogtooth.

The Cathedral Museum is well worth a visit for it contains much that is both interesting and instructive about Dunblane and district. During the very early fifteenth century Bishop Findlay Dermoch built a single arch bridge across the Allan at Dunblane. That bridge still survives though widened and probably strengthened. It is fortunate for Dunblane that the A9 practically by-passes the town, certainly that part containing the Cathedral and the older houses, leaving it in peace to enjoy the fruits of age and dignity.

While the A9 heads north-east, another road, the A84, heads north-westwards through the village of Doune towards Callander and the blue peak of Ben Ledi beyond which is MacGregor country. Doune is a nice little village that was once famous as the home of the finest inlaid pistols. This almost unique industry survived for a time after the Disarming Acts of 1745 and today these firearms are highly valued collectors' pieces. Many of these finely engraved pistols can be seen at the Museum of Antiquities in Edinburgh and the Royal Scottish Museum in Glasgow. Doune Castle, one of the finest Scottish castles, is close to the village and is open to the public. It stands right above the junction of the Teith and Ardoch Burn.

CALLANDER. Population 1,761

The motorist looking for peace and quiet will do well to turn left in Doune and then right on to the B8032 for the pleasant but not spectacular journey to Callander, following the south bank of the River Teith, which is here joined by the River Leny flowing from Loch Lubnaig through the picturesque Pass of Leny. West of the town is some of the most beautiful country in Scotland, not quite Highland, yet with nothing of the Lowlands about the landscape.

Callander, a Burgh, is in an enviable situation under the shadow of Ben Ledi and at the entrance to the Trossachs. Ben Ledi means the Hill of God. The town itself is a pleasant enough resort but it is as the centre from which to explore the surrounding country that Callander obtains its prominence—that and its fame as Tannochbrae in the television series, 'Doctor Finlay's Casebook'. There are many lovely walks to be made from Callander among which may be mentioned the following: the Red Well, Bracklinn Falls, the Wishing Well, along the River Teith and many more farther afield. This appears to be as far west as the Romans penetrated and here they left the remnants of a camp which can still be inspected by those with a liking for Roman history. From Callander the A84 continues northwards to the Breadalbane Hills and the Highlands, while westwards the A821 dives straight into the Trossachs, a word which means Rugged Country.

THE TROSSACHS

This truly delightful piece of country has been much commercialised
and probably receives more visitors than any other part of Scotland.
In spite of this drawback it is beyond compare for its rugged, heavily
wooded scenery, more especially where the road comes to an end at
the eastern end of Loch Katrine and the steamers leave for the trip
along this most beautiful of Lochs. The road from Callander follows
the north bank of Loch Venachar to Loch Achray and the Achray
Forest. Ben Ledi and Ben Venue tower over the Trossachs giving the
final touch to a superb picture.

From Loch Katrine the road turns south and, climbing hills through
the Achray Forest, which is a portion of the huge reserve of the Queen
Elizabeth National Forest Park, passes the David Marshall Lodge where
at the highest point of this quite short journey is a parking plot and a
lodge where coffee can be obtained while enjoying the magnificent
views; foresters are also there to enlighten the inquisitive. Six miles
from Loch Katrine the road drops down to Aberfoyle.

ABERFOYLE. Population 700

Aberfoyle is one of those attractive little places that is the centre for
some delightful runs. It also has the distinction of being connected
with Sir Walter Scott and his *Lady of the Lake*, as well as *Rob Roy*.
A secondary road from Aberfoyle runs alongside Loch Ard, Loch
Chon, touches the south of Loch Katrine and follows the north bank
of Loch Arklet to the east bank of Loch Lomond, where there is an
hotel and superb views of this famous Loch from a point that very few
people will have visited. The hotel, where the road ends, is almost
opposite the Cobbler. This is one of the runs that the discerning
motorist will not regret. North of this point, on an island in the Loch,
is a ruined castle, and on the east bank of the Loch is Rob Roy's cave.

Three miles east of Aberfoyle is Lake Menteith, with the ruins of
Inchnaholme Priory on an island. This is under the control of the
Dept. of Environment and a ferry runs from Port of Menteith. There
is also a castle ruin on another island. This road, the A873, returns to
Stirling through the village of Thornhill.

Northwards from Callander there is only one road which runs,
closely crowded by the River Teith, through the Pass of Leny into
Rob Roy country. The road closely follows Loch Lubnaig with
Beinn Each, Ben Ledi and Benvane towering overhead. The scenery
changes as one proceeds northwards—the green straths have been
left behind and ahead are the hills and mountains. Rob Roy was
immortalised by Scott but his grave can be visited in the churchyard
of the tiny village of Balquhidder at the eastern end of Loch Voil.
Turn left at the hamlet of Kingshouse a few miles beyond Loch
Lubnaig. The nine-mile trip to the end of this narrow road along
Loch Voil and Loch Doine under the shadow of Ben More and a

score of other hills, all over 2,000 feet, is more than worth while.
Three miles south of Kingshouse, at Strathyre, is another Forest
Centre in the Strathyre Forest.

Three miles north of Kingshouse is the water-ski centre at
Lochearnhead, at the western end of Loch Earn. Close by on the
south bank of the Loch are the Castle of Edinaple and the Falls of
Edinaple. The Castle, a fifteenth-century baronial mansion, is not open
to the public but a good view can be had from the road. The Falls
can be approached by a footpath through Edinaple Farm, and they
are only a few yards from the road. Lochearnhead itself is a growing
holiday centre at the southern end of the extremely rugged and
beautiful Glen Ogle through which the river and the road crowd each
other through the rocks and woods. It is also the junction of the A84
with the A85, which follows the north bank of Loch Earn to Comrie.
The discerning motorist, with an eye open for the beauties of the
secondary roads, will take the road along the south bank of the Loch
through woods and two tiny hamlets to join the A85 at the village of
St. Fillans on the east end of Loch Earn.

Eastwards along the A85. Comrie is the next village with two
distinctive features : it is on the geological fault known as the
Highland Border Fault and is the earthquake centre of Scotland. This
does not worry Comrieans or holidaymakers, for the last really severe
shock was in the 1830s. It is also at the western end of Strathearn,
that broad belt, widening towards the east, of green fields and lowland
aspect, northwards of which the Romans never penetrated. There is a
side-road northwards out of Comrie which leads, in a very short
distance, to a rugged and wild glen with a waterfall known as the
Devil's Cauldron. On the eastern outskirts of the village are two
monuments—both are copies of Cleopatra's Needle and both
commemorate Scottish Generals who fought in the Egyptian wars.

CRIEFF. Population 5,773

Following the River Earn through the wide and pleasant Strath the
road soon reaches Crieff, a delightful little town built on a hill and on
the edge of the hills south of Glen Almond. Nearby are the Falls of
Kiltie and some magnificent walks in green country. Three miles
south-east is Muthill Old Church and Tower in the charge of the
Dept. of Environment, who also control the fine old Chapel at
Tullibardine, three miles farther south near Kinkell Bridge. Some three
miles south of Crieff are the very fine gardens of Drummond Castle
which are opened to the public on certain occasions. A little farther
east are the ruins of Innerpeffray Church in charge of the Dept. of
Environment.

From Crieff to Perth, a matter of seventeen miles, the road skirts the
northern edge of Strathearn through well-wooded agricultural
country ; only one place of interest is passed six miles east of Crieff,

where a side-road on the north side leads to Fowlis Wester and the
Kirk of St. Bean. This little kirk dates from the thirteenth century but
stands on the site of something a great deal more ancient, embedded
in one wall was found the Pictish Stone now standing by the vestry.
This is possibly the only kirk remaining in Northern Scotland that still
has pre-Reformation paintings and decoration; it is remarkable that
St. Bean should have escaped the post-Reformation destruction. The
village was once of some importance and the road to Perth a busy
drove road. A few miles nearer Perth Methven Castle will be noticed
on a hill-top just north of the road, making a fine and typically
Scottish picture.

Perth

Status: City.
How to Get There: (*By Rail*). Excellent service from Glasgow,
from Edinburgh with a through service from London, Aberdeen and
Inverness.

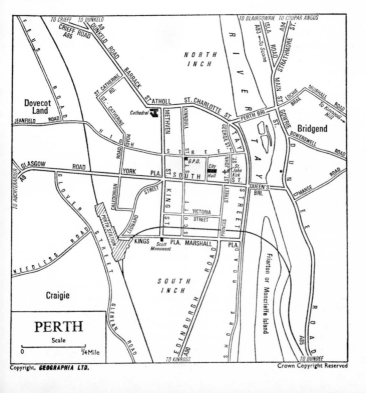

(*By Road.*) Excellent bus service from Edinburgh, Glasgow and the surrounding area.

Population: 43,000.

Early Closing Day: Wednesday.

Post Office: Junction of Meal Vennel and South Street.

Tourist Information Centre: Marshall Place.

Places of Worship: St. John's Kirk, St. Ninian's Cathedral.

Parking Places: Barrack Street, Charlotte, Bridge Lane, Tay Street, Scott Street, Canal Street, King Street, Kings Place, St. Cathrine's Road.

Cinemas: Playhouse, Murray Street, Odeon, Kinnoull Street.

Theatre: Perth Theatre, High Street.

Parks and Open Spaces: The North Inch, The South Inch.

Newspapers: Perthshire Advertiser (Wednesday and Saturday), Dundee Courier (daily), People's Journal (weekly).

Other Amenities: Black Watch Museum, Balhousie Castle, swimming, ice rink, golf, tennis, fishing, conferences and exhibitions, Museum and Art Gallery, George Street, Bell Indoor Sports Centre.

MANY MOTORISTS WILL travel to Perth from the south via the Queensferry Bridge and so miss the finest introduction to the Highlands. The age-old historical route to Northern Scotland is via Stirling and Strathallan and Strathearn to Perth; on reaching the high ground just south of the River Tay stop and take in the view the Romans must have seen when first they approached the Highlands. To the north and west is a ring of hills continuing as far as the eye can see, below are the green fields, the woods and the wide pleasant banks of the slow and widening River Tay. In the midst of this lovely scene is Perth, the southern gateway to the Highlands; a hundred miles north is Inverness, the northern gateway, and between them the Great North Road has for many centuries carried the armies of attack and defence, the commerce and the comings and goings of important personages that have one and all effected the history of Scotland.

Perth is in some ways the most important city of Scotland. It was the capital long before Edinburgh; it was a Pictish centre and today is one of the five cities entitled to call its civic head Lord Provost; in addition it ranks before all other cities excepting Edinburgh. The old name of Perth was St. John's Town and the centre of modern Perth is the Kirk of St. John, the steeple of which can be seen for a great distance. Although a great deal of this church was rebuilt in the eighteenth century there is some thirteenth-century work still surviving, chiefly the nave and transept; the choir and steeple are fifteenth. It is one of the quirks of fortune that here in St. John's, where John Knox preached and where the Reformation and subsequent

South Uist

Glen Affric

Crathes Castle, Tower Room

destruction of church property began, here survives the only collection of pre-Reformation church plate in any church and possibly in Scotland. This collection can be seen in a glass case in the kirk.

Apart from St. John's there are few ancient buildings to remind one of the historic past. That fine stretch of turf alongside the River Tay, known as the North Inch, holds, perhaps, more history than one might suppose. Many notable events have been held on this fine greensward, of which the most unusual took place in the 1390s, when two groups of Highlanders from the Clans Kay and Chattan agreed to settle their differences by battle between thirty men from each Clan. The whole town, including many notables and foreigners, were among the spectators of the fight which ensued. Scott has told the story in his *Fair Maid of Perth*. Apparently only one man got away unwounded. It was on the South Inch that cricket was born in Scotland; in the very early 1800s a regiment of Hussars were stationed here and turned the South Inch into a cricket pitch.

Perth has a fine and attractive river frontage, two bridges across the Tay and a port that does a considerable trade. The Mercat Cross with indicator and the Binns Monument, all on Kinnoull Hill, can be the venue for a quiet afternoon's walk. Across the river, two miles north at Scone, is the Palace and Gardens of Scone which are under the auspices of the National Trust for Scotland; here race-meetings, etc., are held. Scone is the site of the ancient capital where the Scottish kings were crowned and it was from here that Edward Ist took the Stone of Scone, on which the kings were crowned, to Westminster. There seems some doubt whether or not this rough, uncarved and undecorated lump of old red sandstone was in fact the king's seat of very ancient lineage.

Four miles south-east of Perth is Elcho Castle, on the south bank of the Tay and in the hands of the Dept. of Environment. This is well worth a visit as is Huntingtower Castle, two miles west of the city and administered by the same authority. South of Perth, beyond the Bridge of Earn, is the fine picturesque Glen Farg, with a village at the southern end, spelt Glenfarg. This road continues to Loch Leven and Kinross.

Seven roads radiate from Perth, a pointer to the importance of the city's position. Eastwards the Dundee road follows the green and pleasant, also rich agriculturally, strip of land along the north bank of the Firth of Tay known as the Carse of Gowrie. Being protected by the Sidlaw Hills to the north this carse is extremely fertile and for that reason is the site of a string of mansions and castles.

COUPAR ANGUS. Population 2,042

The next road leaves Perth via Scone and travels through a pretty wooded countryside north of the Sidlaw Hills and hemmed in by the outliers of the Grampians to the west and north. This is another

D

fertile valley that leads to the nice old town of Coupar Angus,
built largely of red sandstone and sited by the little River Isla at the
eastern end of the long fertile Howe of Strathmore. The ruins of the
Abbey, founded in 1164, are small but conspicuous, while the
Tolbooth of 1769 has been renovated but retains its attractiveness
and is the centre of a very pleasant little shopping centre. Five miles
farther is the village of Meigle, on the border of Perthshire and very
close to Glamis Castle and village, which will be dealt with in another
section. Meigle has a fine museum of Pictish sculptures.

BLAIRGOWRIE. Population 5,204

The third road from Perth heads almost due north. It is the A93 and
beyond Blairgowrie passes through magnificent scenery as it plunges
straight into the Grampians, only being turned off its northward course
when it meets the heights of the Cairngorms, where it turns east
through Braemar to Aberdeen. Blairgowrie, which was anciently Blair
in Gowrie to distinguish it from Blair in Atholl, sits in a very beautiful
position right on the edge of the Grampians and the rich lands of
Strathmore. As a shopping centre and tourist resort it takes a high
place but it is the superb country around, and the extreme variety of
the country, that really gives Blairgowrie its reputation.

At the village of Meikleour near Blairgowrie is a beech hedge of
titanic proportions and very real beauty. In the area there are several
castles worthy of note. At about the half-way point between Perth and
Blairgowrie is Stobhall Castle, which overlooks the Tay and dates from
the eleventh century. It was the home of the Drummond family. Three
miles north of Blairgowrie is Craighall, the home of the Rattray
family. This mansion sits precariously on the edge of a precipice high
above the narrow gorge through which flows the Ericht—the position
is unique and very beautiful. Newton Castle, the home of the Chief
of the Clan Macpherson, is at the top of Newton Street in
Blairgowrie. It was sacked by Montrose in 1645 so it probably dates
from the sixteenth century or earlier. Glasclune Castle stands on a
hill overlooking the Lornty Burn, some two miles north-west of
Blairgowrie; this is a favourite spot for picnickers and is on the
foothills of the outlying Grampians. Four miles west of the town is
Clunie Loch, and on an island is Clunie Castle, built in 1485. The
first castle here was erected in the ninth century by Kenneth McAlpin.
Right on the northern edge of Perthshire the A93 negotiates the
Devil's Elbow after passing through the magnificent scenery of
Glenshee, where a number of heights of 3,000 feet are within view
and the road itself rises to over 2,000 feet at the Chair-Lift. It is
interesting to remember that one man has climbed all the peaks in
Scotland of over 3,000 feet, and there are well over 500 of them; in
consequence of this marathon feat all heights over 3,000 feet are
known as Munroes after the man who accomplished it.

DUNKELD. Population 1,064. City and Burgh

The fourth road radiating from Perth is the Great North Road, now known as the A9 in Scotland and the A1 in England. It crosses the wide western end of Strathmore to enter the lovely little village and City of Dunkeld, where every visitor should be prepared to spend a day, for this very small place has more to show than many a larger town.

The Cathedral of Dunkeld, dedicated to St. Columba, is without doubt one of the most beautiful ruins in Scotland and is well cared for by the Dept. of Environment. Although early records are scarce it is probable that the Cathedral is on the site of an early Culdee Monastery. It is known that St. Columba's relics were transferred here from the Island of Iona in the ninth century and so it is reasonable to suppose that Dunkeld was already a religious centre of some importance. Today the Cathedral sits close to the Tay, which here is assuming the mantle of a mountain stream, shaded by trees on the rich lawns which surround it. Close by is the bridge erected in 1809 by Telford. Although most of this very ancient Cathedral is partially in ruins the choir is still used as the Parish Church.

The National Trust for Scotland owns twenty houses in Cathedral Street and High Street; they largely date from the rebuilding after the Battle of Dunkeld in 1689; these are a charming set of old houses and should not be missed. Stanley Hill, another National Trust property, is a wooded mound behind the old village of Dunkeld which provides a background of woodland and adds considerably to the overall beauty of the old village. Lady Charlotte's Cave and Craige Barnes View are on the wooded hill north of Dunkeld, while The Hermitage, National Trust property, is a viewpoint overlooking the River Braan, these are all points of great natural beauty.

The twelve miles of good road between Dunkeld and Blairgowrie skirts the foothills of the Grampians and overlooks the broad Strathmore as it follows a stream which joins five lochs. At various points side-roads take off into the hills or across the straths. These are almost always worth while especially for the adventurous motorist; for the walker the country north and west of Dunkeld is wide open and inviting.

Westwards from Dunkeld the A822 follows the River Braan through the narrow Strathbraan and some glorious scenery for about eight miles to a turn-off north to Aberfeldy through Glen Cochill, or southwards through Glen Almond (the Sma'Glen), a steep-sided and hill road, to Crieff.

PITLOCHRY. Population 2,501

Pitlochry is a pleasant little Highland village, for it sits at the confluence of the River Tummel and Loch Faskally, while Ben Vrackie, Creag Dhubh and Meall a'Charra tower overhead on three sides. A little north of the village is the National Trust property known as the Linn of Tummel, which is about fifty acres in extent along the Rivers Tummel and Garry; this is a particularly lovely spot with some fine views of both rivers. Just north of the village on the east side of the road is the Black Spout, a double waterfall. It is very close to the road andis well worth viewing.

ABERFELDY. Population 1,469

From Ballinluig, four miles south of Pitlochry, a road takes off westwards to Aberfeldy, a small tourist resort and market. On the way it passes Grandtully Castle and Church, which are rewarding. Close to Aberfeldy is Menzies Castle, a very interesting ruin and of very considerable age. One of General Wade's finest bridges was built across the River Tay at Aberfeldy in the late 1700s, and it is in use today. A mile or so south of the village are the Moness Falls, which are very fine and in glorious country. From Aberfeldy there are two roads westwards. One goes south-west along the north bank of Loch Tay to the western Highlands, passing in the shadow of Ben Lawers and the National Trust area of many acres of mountains and glens. This is a very scenic road and brings the motorist to Killin and Crianlarich. The other strikes north-westwards to Loch Tummel and the Road to the Isles. This road, famous in song and story, can be joined at the Linn of Tummel north of Pitlochry. It then follows the north bank of Loch Tummel, past the Bridge of Tummel and along the north bank of Loch Rannoch to Rannoch Station on the Highland Railway, where it finishes except for the keen walker who may be able to follow the ancient track, now sadly overgrown, westwards. From Loch Tay and from Loch Tummel and Rannoch there are side-roads into the hills north of Loch Tay which includes Glen Lyon, or on to the rather bleak Rannoch Moor; these side-roads generally have some unexpected rewards.

THE PASS OF KILLIECRANKIE

Seven miles north of Pitlochry on the Great North Road one comes to one of the most famous spots in Scotland, the Pass of Killiecrankie, where in 1689 the English troops of William of Orange suffered one of the heaviest defeats at the hands of the Highlanders. The scene is a remarkably beautiful gorge on one of Scotland's most beautiful streams, the River Garry. There is an Information Centre and café, etc., and the whole area is well worth an afternoon. This property is in the hands of the National Trust for Scotland.

Three miles north of the Pass is Blair Atholl and Blair Castle. The village sits comfortably in the Valley of the River Garry and looks after its visitors with a friendly air. The country around is splendid, with the rugged Glen Garry a little farther north. Blair Castle, has been the home of the Dukes of Atholl for many centuries; the Tower,

which is the oldest surviving portion, was built in 1269. The Castle
contains a remarkable collection of arms, period furniture and
interesting historical relics of every kind. The Castle is open to the
public, who are conducted around the many rooms by a guide.
Three miles north of Blair Castle, at the village of Calvine, there is a
quite lovely footpath walk to the Falls of Bruar on the Bruar Water,
descending from the north to join the Garry; in addition there is the
museum of the Clan Daunachaich.

From Blair Atholl northwards the Great North Road follows the
railway through Glen Garry and the Pass of Drumochter to the county
boundary, Loch Ericht and Inverness. This is the route that General
Wade took when he built his great north road in the late 1700s; it can
still be followed in many places on foot, generally on the east side
of the A9, and many remains of his bridges can still be seen. About
thirteen miles north of Blair Atholl there is a large and prominent stone
on the north side of the road; this is named Wade's Stone and marks
the route of his road.

The fifth road from Perth follows the northern hills along the edge
of the strath to Crieff. The sixth follows the south of the same strath
and the northern edge of the Ochils to Auchterarder, the Allan Water
and Dunblane.

Inveraray

Status: Royal Burgh.
How to Get There: (*By Road*). Twice daily coach service from
Glasgow, connections to all important centres.
Population: 600.
Early Closing Day: Wednesday.
Post Office: Sub-Post Office only.
Tourist Information Centre: The car park at foot of Front Street.
Places of Worship: Parish Church, All Saints', Episcopal. Some
other denominations have places of worship.
Parking Places: Free parking with certain restrictions.
Other Amenities: Sea, loch and river fishing, Auchindrain Museum,
Crarae Gardens. Shinty is played here. Inveraray will be remembered
for the historic buildings and the magnificent countryside.

ALTHOUGH MANY PLACES in Argyllshire and Kintyre can be
reached by steamer there are only three road routes that need to be
taken account of by the motorist, by Tarbet at the north end of Loch
Lomond, by Crianlarich from Perth or Stirling and by Kinlochleven
from Fort William and the north.

From Tarbet on the Dunbartonshire border the motorist travels through absolutely first-class Highland scenery for about twenty-five miles to Inveraray. After rounding the north end of Loch Lomond, Glen Croe, in the shadow of Ben Arthur, better known as the Cobbler, can be enjoyed before the stiff climb up the Rest and be Thankful, from the summit of which there are truly magnificent views. Then comes Glen Kinglas and a pleasant journey around the north end of Loch Fyne, known as the deepest sea loch in Scotland, and on the banks of which sits Inveraray. On the way there are several side-roads for the adventurous motorist. From Perth the road runs west through Crieff and Lochearnhead to Crianlarich; from Stirling north-west through Callander and past Loch Lubnaig to join the road from Perth at Lochearnhead, from where they proceed together along the rugged Glen Ogle to Crianlarich. This little place has a very special air about it, an atmosphere of seeing the traveller on towards the wilder country to the north and west; this is partly due to the railway which runs northwards to Fort William and Mallaig. Before reaching Crianlarich Ben More will be seen towering overhead, with three more Munroes ahead and in view, Beinn Dubhchraig, Ben Oss and Ben Lui crowding the skyline and shouting of more to come. From Crianlarich one can turn south past the Falls of Falloch and through the Glen of Falloch to Loch Lomond and Tarbet; but the route ahead to Dalmally through the narrow Strath Fillan and the delightful Glen Lochy with 2,000- and 3,000-foot peaks all around is by far the more scenic.

Ben Nevis from Banavie

Five miles after leaving Crianlarich the motorist can turn north through some of the finest of Highland scenery to pass close under Beinn Dorain, one of the most beautiful of Scotland's mountains. This route is well worth while if one turns south-west again at the Bridge of Orchy to travel the length of the rugged and picturesque Glen Orchy with the river of the same name tumbling along beside the road. These two routes join again at Inverlochy, just before Dalmally is reached. From here the road splits, one through the Pass of Brander to Oban and the other southwards along the east bank of Loch Awe to Glen Aray and Inveraray.

Inveraray is the oldest Burgh in Argyllshire and was at one time the county town. There has been a castle here since at least 1415 when the Campbells arrived, and this family still owns, and often resides, at Inveraray Castle. But long before the days of stone castles and the clan system had evolved this was a Gaelic settlement. To the long peninsula of Kintyre came the Christian Saints from Ireland, first to the island of Iona then to Kintyre; so that today this is a land rich in the monuments of the very distant past. Argyllshire probably holds more of these very ancient relics and monuments than any other county. It always has been predominately Gaelic and still is, for the Scandinavian influence is considerably less here than farther north.

The present town of Inveraray came into existence only a little over two hundred years ago, when the then Duke of Argyll decided to build a new castle where the then village of Inveraray stood. The new town was well planned and the magnificent Castle of Inveraray took shape. The present town is well worth exploring and a plan of the medieval village can be seen at the Castle office. The Old Town House, the Parish Church, the Courthouse and several other buildings are of great interest. The extremely striking view of the north end of Loch Fyne and Duniquaich Hill from the War Memorial on the waterfront is one of the best features of a town that is full of such features.

The Castle of Inveraray. although only two hundred years old, contains a magnificent collection of Scottish arms of many kinds, an equally fine collection of period furniture, tapestries, pictures and historical relics of the Clan Campbell covering many centuries. There are few finer castles of this type to be seen in Scotland. It is open to the public.

Campbeltown

Status: Royal Burgh.
How to Get There: *(By Air)*. Forty minutes from Glasgow to Machrihanish Airport.
(By Sea). From Ardrossan via Lochranza in Arran by steamer to Claonaig.
(By Road). By coach and bus from Glasgow via Inveraray

Population: 6,500
Early Closing Day: Wednesday.
Post Office: Main Street.
Tourist Information Centre: Head of the Pier.
Place of Worship: The Highland Parish Church of Scotland.
A few other denominations have places of worship.
Parking Places: Street parking with restrictions.
Cinemas: The Rex, Hall Street, The Cinema, Hall Street.
Parks and Open Spaces: Kintyre Park, Kinloch Park.
Newspaper: Campbeltown Courier (Thursday).
Other Amenities: Tennis, golf, bowls, swimming and children's
pool, rowing and sailing, salmon and trout fishing, walking, regattas,
concerts, pipe band and Highland dancing, dancing at Victoria Hall
and Studio Ballroom, High Street.

KNAPDALE, KINTYRE AND CAMPBELTOWN

ARGYLLSHIRE SOUTH OF Inveraray may be divided into three
portions. The extreme southern part of this long peninsula is known
as Kintyre in which is the one town of Campbeltown. This is a
pleasant land of low hills and green valleys with a fine green coastal
strip, treeless on the Atlantic side but rich and beautiful above
Kilbrannan Sound with the hills of Arran seeming so close across
the narrow strip of water. The Mull of Kintyre, the most southern
point and well below Glasgow, is a wild and almost desolate spot with
attractions all its own as one looks across to Ireland or straight out
into the Atlantic. The first is the way the missionaries came, the
second is the way the Highlanders went after the clearances and
during the years of depression. Here it is said the Wildcat and the
Golden Eagle can still be seen.

Campbeltown sits safely and comfortably at the head of the short
sea loch that provides shelter and a perfect harbour. A holiday resort
with much to offer the visitor as well as a fishing port of some renown,
Campbeltown can be a gay and most pleasant spot. At the Old Quay
Head is Campbeltown Cross, a very fine fifteenth-century cross with
Celtic decorations. At the mouth of the Loch is the tiny island of
Davaar, which can be reached on foot at low tide, but care is needed
to ensure a safe return. On the island is a cave on one wall of which
an artist, Archibald MacKinnon, painted a picture of the Crucifixion in
1887. This is a truly remarkable picture and is seen by many hundreds
every year. Over the town two hills stand guard, Bengullion and
Knockscalbert; on the former is the Piper's Cave which has never
been completely explored. The story tells that in the long ago a Piper,
having been jilted by his betrothed, marched into the cave with his
dog and playing his pipes. Some days later the dog reappeared at
Southend, ten miles away. The Piper was never seen again. From
Southend village a narrow road runs south through some of the wildest

scenery in Kintyre to the lighthouse on the Mull; it is better to walk
the last mile since there is little room at the far end of the road. The
scenery here is awe-inspiring when the western gales are blowing.

Northwards from Campbeltown the main road travels up the
Atlantic coast; on the hilltop outside the town is a car park for the
enjoyment of the wonderful views. This is a treeless but magnificent
coastline with rocks of fantastic shape; at Mousdale they stand like
sentinels, the drift being almost vertical. Killean is a nice little village
with a fine church ruin and the vault of the Largie family. At various
points there are grand views of Gigha Island and the tiny Cara Island,
both with ancient ruins.

TARBERT

Several more villages occur before the run along the banks of West
Loch Tarbert to the fine fishing village of Tarbert, with the old Castle
overlooking the harbour from its hilltop position. From West Loch
Tarbert there are ferry services to Islay and Jura off the west coast,
and from Tarbert itself there are steamer services to Gourock and
trips on Loch Fyne. There is an interesting old story about Tarbert
which tells how the chief of these parts rashly promised an invader
all the land he could sail around. This worthy pirate sailed from West
Loch Tarbert around the Mull and up the Kilbrennan Sound to
Tarbert. There he had his ship manhandled over the short mile to
West Loch Tarbert, and so became Lord of Kintyre. The other road,
along the Kilbrannan Sound, passes two delightful villages, Carradale
and Skipness, as well as much fine scenery.

From Tarbert one can take the main road along Loch Fyne and
enjoy the very grand views of the Loch itself as well as paying a
visit to the Forest Gardens at Crarae. The pleasanter road of the two
is B8024, around the hilly Knapdale Peninsula, which enables one to
see the many monuments including the Castle and Chapel of St.
Brenda, of date 1100, the Kilberry Stone, the Vitrified Fort and many
others. This second-class road along the Sound of Jura enables one
to enjoy finer scenery and much less traffic. At the wide sea Loch
Caolisport the road turns along the lochside to join the main road
south of Ardrishaig, where a swing bridge takes the road across the
Crinan Canal which joins the Sound of Jura with Loch Fyne. In six
miles Lochgilphead is reached.

LOCHGILPHEAD. Population 1,208

Lochgilphead is a good centre from which to explore the country
between Loch Caolisport and Inveraray. This very lovely piece of
country can be seen in one trip but it certainly warrants a few days.
Take the road south from Lochgilphead along the banks of Loch Fyne
to Ardrishaig, where the canal should be seen. It was constructed in
the last few years of the 1700s and for the whole of its length it

travels through some of the most beautiful country in Argyllshire.
Continue south for three miles to the B8024 turn right and pass
Loch Arail to the hamlet of Achahoish, then turn right again on to a
narrow road that follows the north bank of Loch Caolisport through
wooded country to Kilmory, where there is a fine stone Cross and
remarkable views of the many islands off the coast. The track then
follows the coast to Castle Sween on the sea Loch Sween and under
the care of the Dept. of Environment. It continues along the rugged
coastline through woods to Knapdale Forest, where it joins the B8025
to Tayvallich and that long strip of green land that finishes at
Keillmore with a track to the Island of Danna, or to the Point of Knap.
The return to Lochgilphead is by the same road to the B841 and the
A816.

North of the B841 and the A816 is not strictly Knapdale; it is,
however, well worthy of exploration. Take the A816 out of
Lochgilphead towards Kilmartin, stopping to explore the interesting
features around this little-known corner; there are the following all
under the Dept. of Environment. Dunadd Fort; Kilmartin Stones in the
churchyard at Kilmartin; Temple Wood, Circle and Cist Kilmartin;
Ri Cruin Cairn, Kilmartin; Ballygowan, Cup and Ring Marked Stones,
Kilmartin; Glebe Cairn, Kilmartin. There are a number of other Dept. of
Environment features in the immediate vicinity. Nearer the coast there
is a Broch at Ardfuir. Just beyond is Carnassarie Castle, also under
the Dept. of Environment.

This road continues northwards along the broken coastline across
green valleys and under the hills that break up this corner of
Argyllshire. It passes close to the southern end of Loch Awe, and
returns to the coast which it more or less follows to Kilninver and
Oban. Countless islands will have been seen offshore and the views,
both seawards and inland, are superb. This is one of the loveliest runs
in Argyllshire.

A little north of Kilmartin the B840 forks to the right and follows
the east bank of the lovely Loch Awe, by two castles and through
much wooded country, to its junction with the A819 and a return
to Lochgilphead through Inveraray.

Cowal and the Island of Bute
Dunoon and Rothesay

Dunoon

Status: Burgh.
How to Get There: By rail from Glasgow to Gourock, car
ferry from Gourock. By road via Arrochar and 'Rest and be Thankful'.
Population: 9,333.

Early Closing Day: Wednesday.
Post Office: Argyll Street.
Tourist Information Centre: Pier Esplanade.
Newspaper: Dunoon Observer (Friday).
Cinema: La Scala, Argyll Street.
Other Amenities: Sports stadium, golf, bowls, tennis, crazy golf, fishing, yachting, rowing and motor boats, indoor swimming pool.

Rothesay

How to Get There: By ferry from Colintraive in Argyll. By train from Glasgow to Wemyss Bay then by car ferry. By coach from Glasgow to Wemyss Bay, then ferry.
Population: 7,656.
Tourist Information Centre: Information Bureau, Main Pier Approach.
Newspaper: Buteman and Rothesay Express (Friday).

THE ONLY ROAD into the peninsula of Cowal is the Arrochar Inveraray road which, almost on the west shore of Loch Fyne, forks south into Cowal and eventually becomes three roads which cover the full length of the peninsula and give access to the ferry for the Island of Bute. Dunoon is the only town on the peninsula and Rothesay the only one on the Island of Bute. Both are capital and popular resorts with all the usual amenities. The usual approach is by steamer from Gourock across the Firth of Clyde, for the road journey from Glasgow is about eighty-five miles, while the sea route is no more than six. Many of the steamers are car ferries and this route affords many grand views of the Clyde, the Firth, Loch Long and Holy Loch. Steamers also sail from Glasgow, and Wemyss Bay.

The Cowal peninsula is shaped like a pear with the narrow end at the north between Loch Goil and Loch Fyne; on the east side it is bounded by Loch Goiland and Loch Long and on the west by Loch Fyne. On the southern end a great bite has been taken out, forming the Kyles of Bute, and into this gap the island of Bute inserts nearly half its length. The Kyles of Bute and Loch Striven flow northwards into the peninsula so that the southern half of Cowal is in reality three peninsulas. Dunoon is the only town of any size and is one of the most popular holiday centres. From it coaches leave on tours not only in the peninsula but to many places farther afield; in fact, Dunoon is noted for its coach tours.

Within Cowal there are three roads from north to south and one from the head of the Holy Loch to the head of the Kyles of Bute.

Coming into Cowal from the north the road forks at the village of Strachur, the left-hand road going through Glen Branter and

Glenbranter Forest, where Sir Harry Lauder had his home, to the very
beautiful Loch Eck, from where a narrow road strikes off through Glen
Finart to Loch Fyne and then around the coast to the Holy Loch
and north to Loch Eck. This is a very scenic run.

From the head of the Holy Loch the only east–west road leaves by
way of Glen Lean, around the head of Loch Striven to the Clachan of
Glendaruel and northwards through the lovely Glen Ghleann to
Loch Fyne and the main road at Strachur on Loch Fyne. The ferry
for Bute leaves from Ardentraive, some six miles south of the junction
of the east–west and north–south road.

From a little farther down Loch Fyne another road follows the
picturesque shores closely as far as Otter Ferry and then continues
farther inland to the tip of the peninsula and Port Driseach. The
peninsula of Cowal is largely a land of hills, not as high as the main
Highlands, cut up by glens, lochs and rivers into an everchanging land
of great beauty without the gaunt ruggedness of the Highlands
proper.

Among the many places of interest the following castles are all well
worth viewing: Dunoon Castle, of date some time previous to 1563
when Mary Queen of Scots visited it; Toward Castle, at the most
southerly point some twelve miles south of Dunoon, dating from the
late fifteenth century; Carrick Castle, on the west bank of Loch Goil,
another fifteenth-century castle that was partially destroyed during
the late 1600s, which is best reached from Lochgoilhead; Castle
Lachlan, on the east bank of Loch Fyne, close to the village of Castle
Lachlan; it dates from about 1430.

ROTHESAY AND THE ISLE OF BUTE

The Isle of Bute is not a very large one, perhaps eighteen miles by
six or seven at the widest point, but within this quite small area
there is a diversity of countryside that is quite surprising. In the
north are the moorlands and most of the hills, admittedly not very
high but picturesque for all that, and delightfully cut up with glens
that make good picnicking sites. The south is far greener and more
fertile, being generally of a lower altitude. Probably Bute's most
popular features are the number of fine, sandy and safe swimming
beaches from Ettrick Bay on the west coast to Ascog Bay on the
east; between these two are many more, including Scalpsie, where
the sand is red-coloured against a backcloth of green. From a high
point on the road close to Scalpsie is the finest view in, or from, Bute.
It takes in the widening Firth of Clyde with the hills of Ayrshire and
Galloway on the left and the outstanding peaks of Arran on the right.
Dunagoil, near Carroch Head at the extreme southern point of the
island, is, perhaps, the loveliest and least frequented beach of all.
Immediately to the east is Little Cumbrae and a mile or two to the

north Great Cumbrae ; these two little islands sit in the Firth about half-way between the mainland and Bute. Great Cumbrae is inhabited and sports the very pleasant little town of Millport.

ROTHESAY

As the largest town and the county town of Buteshire Rothesay has over the years become a most popular holiday resort and mecca for day-trippers as well as a calling point for the many Clyde steamers that ply up and down the Firth, the Kyles of Bute and the many lochs around this most broken coastline from Campbeltown and the Kintyre peninsula to Dunoon and the River Clyde.

There is not much that Rothesay does not offer the visitor. Steamer trips through magnificent scenery ; quiet little places a few miles away for those seeking peace, and the more modern amenities for the younger and noisier holiday-maker are at Rothesay itself. For the amateur walker Bute is a fine stamping ground where hills of 500 and 600 feet may be tackled easily and safely, or the green glens offer a delightful alternative. South of Rothesay there are several lochs that always add to the interest of any walk. On the west coast, off St. Ninian's Bay, which is known as the Cookle Shore, is the island of Inchmarnock, known as the Drunkards' Isle, as apparently in days gone by those who had one over the eight were despatched to this little island to cool off.

The Isle of Arran

How to Get There: (*By Sea*). Steamer service from Ardrossan and Claonaig (summer). Buses meet the steamers and convey passengers to their destination on Arran. Brodick and Lochranza are the two ports.
Population: 3,700.
Early Closing Day: Wednesday.
Post Offices: At Brodick, Lochranza and a number of the many coastal villages.
Tourist Information Office: Near entrance to Brodick Pier.
Parking Places: Official car parks. At Brodick Pier to Pellegrini's Café and by putting green. At Lochranza, the pier to Bakery.
At Lamlash, close to Ship House. At Whiting Bay, centre of shopping area.
Cinemas: Films are shown occasionally at the Village Halls.
Newspapers: The Buteman, The Ardrossan and Saltcoats Herald (Friday). Arran Banner (monthly).
Other Amenities: Golf, mountaineering, pony trekking, sea angling, loch and burn fishing, water ski-ing, boating and sailing, tennis, bowls, walking.

FOR ITS SMALL size Arran probably has more of beauty and
interest to show the visitor than any other part of Northern Scotland.
At its longest Arran is no more than twenty miles, at its widest no
more than twelve, a road encircles it and two cross the island from
east to west. The northern end is largely composed of hills or
mountains of which the principal are Goatfell, 2,860 feet; Caisteal
Abhail or the Forked Castle, 2,810; Beinn Tarsuinn, 2,700; Cir Mhor
or the Great Comb, 2,610; Beinn Nuis or the Hill of the Human Face,
2,590; Am Binnein or the Small Hill, 2,170; Cioch na h'Oighe or the
Maiden's Breast, 2,168; Beinn a Chliabhain or the Cradled Hill,
2,140; and Suidhe Fhearghas or Fergus's Seat, 2,080. All of these
offer walking of the finest class while some can offer the mountaineer
and rock climber much good sport. And among these mountains and
hills are glens of the most exquisite beauty, much softer than the
Highland glens; in their upper reaches they still contain some
rugged country. Many of the rarer birds can still be seen—the Golden
Eagle has been reported as well as the Hen Harrier. Red Deer are
also fairly common. South of the mountains the moorlands spread
out while the coastline contains an area of exceptionally rich and
verdant land that produces exotic flowers and decorative trees in
abundance, so that in late spring and summer the island becomes a
kaleidoscope of colour around the coast while the bracken of the
lower hills and the greys and blacks of the higher peaks act as a
backcloth and set Arran off to the visitor in the same way that the
Cuillins of Skye do, presenting a picture of fairy-like beauty, although
these two islands are very different in almost every way.

The village of Brodick, which is the chief port of call for passenger
steamers, sits in a superb position at the head of Brodick Bay. Three
of the finest glens open on to the village while the Castle of Brodick,
now under the National Trust for Scotland and open to the public,
keeps watch from its height overlooking the Bay and the village. It
dates from the fourteenth century and contains much that is both
attractive and interesting as well as beautiful. The Castle gardens are
considered among the best in Scotland and are also open to the
public.

Lamlash at the head of Lamlash Bay and protected by Holy Island,
which all but blocks the entrance to the Bay, is the administrative
centre and second port of call for steamers. It is also the
headquarters of the Arran Yacht Club. Apart from the many fine
walks inland from Lamlash, Holy Island can offer a central peak of
1,000 feet from where some wonderful views are to be had; a ferry
operates during the summer months from Lamlash harbour.

Whiting Bay is almost completely modern and well spread out and
offers most of the amenities one could wish for; it is also the centre
for some fine walks—the highest point in the immediate hinterland
is Tighvein, 1,497 feet.

Kildonan is the smallest resort but not the smallest village. It has a fine sandy beach and offshore is Pladda Island, a favourite picnic spot. The village is overlooked by the ruins of a castle and itself overlooks the island of Pladda and, in the distance, Ailsa Craig.

Blackwaterfoot, on the shallow half-moon of Drumadoon Bay, is a great centre for pony trekking and, in addition, is one of the nicest and safest of bathing beaches with a particularly picturesque harbour. There are two caves worth seeing, the King's Cave, two miles north of the village, which came by its name because of associations with Robert the Bruce, and, a mile south of the village in the tiny hamlet of Kilpatrick there is a cave that for many years was the village school.

Lochranza is situated at the head of the sea Loch Ranza and in consequence is another popular tie-up for yachts. The Castle of Lochranza, although dating only from the seventeenth century, is a ruin yet completely dominates the Loch and the village. It is, of course, on the site of a much earlier castle.

The tiny village of Sannox lies along the very shallow Sannox Bay, which is one of the nicest bathing beaches as well as one of the least crowded. A little farther south is Corrie, a very picturesque village of whitewashed cottages, and a favourite with artists. Here again the long sandy beach is a favourite with swimmers and non-swimmers alike.

Among the particular points of interest and beauty are the following: quite a large number of prehistoric remains; hill forts; chambered cairns, etc.; the cell of St. Molaise on Holy Island; Kildonan Castle; Brodick Castle; Lochranza Castle; Highland Mary's Cottage at Lochranza. There are a number of interesting geological features, namely the Fallen Rocks and the Rocking Stone at Sannox, and several others inland. The Arran Gallery in Whiting Bay; coalmine and saltpans at Cock Farm as well as the Limestone Caves and Nabob's Bath at Corrie. There are a number of species of very beautiful stones which can sometimes be found by visitors, and there is a jewellery workshop in Whiting where these, cut and polished, are on show.

Arran has been a populated island since at least the Neolithic immigration from the Mediterranean, and some of their chambered cairns can be seen today. The Romans were here, a fact few people will be aware of, and of course many other nations have contributed to the present blood of Arran, including the Norsemen, who have left their mark in place-names as well as in many ways unseen. While some parts of Northern Scotland can, with some certainty, be pronounced as predominantly Norse, or Celtic, Arran is probably a mixture of all those who in various parts have contributed to the blood of Scotland. Today Arran is almost purely agricultural with the tourist trade a very good second; in consequence it has lost nothing to industrialisation and remains one of the most pleasant and colourful parts of Northern Scotland.

ISLAY

Off the coast of Argyllshire there are many lovely and colourful islands. Some can be visited by regular ferry services and for some a local boat may have to be hired. Apart from Arran and the Isle of Bute, the three largest are Islay, Jura and Mull.

Islay can be visited by steamer from West Loch Tarbert or by air from Renfrew to the Airport at Glenegadale. The west side is generally good agricultural land while the east is hilly and rather more rugged. There are many good beaches in protected coves, while shooting and fishing is a popular pastime.

JURA

Although Jura is almost one with Islay it is a very much more mountainous, wilder and more rugged island and should attract the walker. Craighouse, the port, sits at the south-eastern end. Deer and other wild life form the greatest population of Jura while the coast in many parts is among the most broken and rugged, with plenty of caves. The three Paps of Jura, all over 2,000 feet, are in the south of the island, while in the north between Jura and Scarba is the famous Corryvreckan whirlpool.

MULL

Mull is serviced by steamer from Oban to the port at Craigmore. This is one of those islands that cannot be summed up in a few words; it has good roads which cover most of it yet there is a lot of wild country that only the walker can visit, particularly around Ben More, which is over 3,000 feet high. Along the south coast there is a lot of country that is well away from the road—in every way a delightful holiday island.

At Fionphort a ferry will take the visitor to the island of Iona. Often called the Cradle of Christianity it was here that St. Columba first preached in the sixth century. Columba's Monastery has long since gone but the remains of a later one have been renovated and rebuilt, and Iona may now be regarded as one of the holy places of the world.

The ferry may, when weather permits, be taken to the Isle of Staffa, noted for its famous caves, particularly Fingal's, where the black basalt rises perpendicularly from the ocean to form one of the most remarkable geological formations and astounding pictures. Unfortunately one can no longer land at Staffa.

Oban

Status: Burgh.
How to Get There: (*By Rail*). Regular service from Glasgow.
Connections at Crianlarich for Fort William and Mallaig.
(*By Road.*) Coach service from Glasgow. Daily service to Fort William.
Population: 7,000.
Early Closing Day: Thursday.
Post Office: Albany Street.
Tourist Information Centre: Albany Street.
Places of Worship: Old Parish Church, Church of Scotland.
Several other denominations have places of worship.
Parking Places: Free ; Lochavullin, Stafford Street, Campbell Street.
Small charge ; Ganavan Sands, Dunollie Road, North Pier, Esplanade,
Albany Street.
Cinema: Phoenix, George Street.
Theatres: Concerts and Variety Entertainment. A Repertoire Theatre
Company provide shows.
Parks and Open Spaces: Corran Parks and Esplanade, Dungallan
Parks, Pulpit Hill.
Newspaper: The Oban Times (Thursday)
Other Amenities: Dancing, golf, yachting, swimming, Ganavan
Sands with pavilion and tea room, caravan park and children's
playground, putting, a powerful telescope on the summit of Pulpit Hill.

PROBABLY THE MOST popular approach to Oban will be from
Crianlarich via Tyndrum, where the Fort William and Oban lines of
the Highland Railway are very close together for the last time.
From here the railway and the road travel together down Glen Lochy,
through Dalmally, past the north end of Loch Awe where Kilchurn
Castle, under the Dept. of Environment, should be seen, as should the
Falls of Cruachan at the entrance to the Pass of Brander under that
most shapely of mountains, Ben Cruachan. Having crossed the
Bridge of Awe, Taynuilt is reached. From the high ground above the
village is a superb view of Loch Etive and Ben Cruachan. The road
and railway follow the same route not far from Loch Etive and finally
along the shore to Connel, which is, unfortunately, distinguished by
an ugly iron bridge over the Falls of Laura. From here it is a green and
pleasant run of under five miles to Oban. A side-road can be taken
over rolling hills from Taynuilt through Glen Lonan to Oban. Some
two miles before entering Oban on the main coast-road is
Dunstaffnage Castle and Chapel, under the Dept. of Environment.
Both are well worth a visit for Dunstaffnage holds one of the finest
positions of any castle in the Western Highlands and from its
battlements a truly magnificent view can be had. Originally it
belonged to the MacDougalls but later came into the possession of

E

the Campbells. It was here that the Stone of Destiny was first housed before its removal to Scone and its final forced removal by Edward I to London. Not very much is known about the Chapel but it has a fine Norman doorway.

Oban is, as has often been asserted, the Gem of the Highlands. Its position is really great, well protected by the hills from the northern winds, protected from the Atlantic gales by the island of Mull and with its immediate shore-line well covered by the small island of Kerrera. Spring growth is phenomenal, and many sub-tropical plants can be cultivated here, while roses and rhododendrons make a particularly fine showing. Oban is, today, the capital of the district known as South Lorn, which lies between Loch Awe, the coast of the Firth of Lorn and Loch Etive. But this was not always so, for Oban is only around 150 years of age. No doubt Dunstaffnage Castle was anciently the capital. The modern town caters for visitors in a big way and remains a very friendly place.

On the highest hill close to Oban is the McCaig Tower, which is very like the Colosseum at Rome. It is an outstanding monument but has no historical value, having been built in the 1890s to relieve unemployment by a citizen of Oban. The outstanding feature of the town is Pulpit Hill, at the south end, and commanding views that have been described as the finest in the United Kingdom. If this is not strictly true it very nearly is. Just off Oban Bay is the island of Kerrera. Green and agriculturally fertile, this little island saw the death of King Alexander II of Scotland in 1249. On it is the rather sad but picturesque ruin of Gylen Castle, which once belonged to the

Iona, Isle of Mull in background

MacDougalls who, in 1647, were driven out by the English troops. The famous Brooch of Lorn was in the Castle when it was burnt and was therefore presumed lost for ever, until in 1823 it turned up in a London auction room and was presented to MacDougall of MacDougall by the Campbells.

Dunollie Castle stands on a bluff just north of the town and was the home of the Lords of Lorn, the MacDougalls, who were finally defeated by King Bruce near the Bridge of Awe in the Pass of Brander. Very close to this bridge in a field on the south side of the river can still be seen the cairns, now grass grown, which mark the graves of those who lost the day. A few miles south of Oban is the tiny hamlet of Kilninver, from where the winding road can be taken through a quiet countryside to the island of Seil by the only bridge which crosses the Atlantic, the Clachan Bridge across the Seil Sound. All around Oban there are side-roads, and one along the west side of Loch Awe is particularly attractive, as is the B840 on the east side. All these side-roads hold surprises and rewards. For the walker this is, perhaps, the finest country in the Western Highlands, not too rough as the central and northern Highlands tend to be, and affording an endless variety of routes of any length desired.

Among the very many places that should not be missed are the St. Conan's Kirk on Loch Awe side and the Power Station in the Pass of Brander. St. Conan's Kirk is named after the Patron Saint of Lorn, who was a pupil of St. Columba in the sixth century. The new kirk, on the site of the old, is a memorial to the Campbells of Innischonain and was not completed until after the first world war; it is a magnificent building of granite from nearby Ben Cruachan, and the roof timbers are from two old battleships. There are many fine relics inside and many features of great interest. The style of architecture is Norman. There are, of course, a great many tours by steamer, by coach and by rail from Oban and the visitor who fails to enjoy this delightful holiday resort will indeed be hard to please.

The road from Fort William and the north encircles that wild and sparsley populated piece of country that is bounded by the coast, Loch Leven, Glen Coe, Glen Orchy, the north end of Loch Awe, the Pass of Brander and Loch Etive. This piece of 'Caledonia stern and wild' is known as North Lorn and is as steeped in history as any part of the Highlands; it is very nearly cut in half by the beautiful Loch Etive which, with Glen Etive, almost reaches Glen Coe in the north.

From Taynuilt the Pass of Brander heads south-east to Loch Awe, passing the power-station and the Falls of Cruachan, both of which should be seen, to arrive at the very tiny village of Lochawe, and, on a small peninsula at the loch side, the ruined castle of Kilchurn, of which there are some very interesting remains. The position and outlook from the castle are the finest attraction of this very beautiful spot, Turning left at Inverlochy the road twists its way through this delightful Glen Orchy to the Bridge of Orchy, where it joins the A82 from Crianlarich. Here a side-road can, with superb scenery, be taken around Loch Tulla to rejoin the main road after about six miles. After passing several lochs the chair-lift to the summit of Meall a Bhuiridh, with the Kingshouse Hotel opposite, is approached, and very shortly the head of Glen Coe appears amid some of the most rugged scenery it is possible to imagine; as a complete contrast the view down Glen Coe is extraordinarily beautiful, while the tops of the mountains are rugged in the extreme the lower parts of the Glen are comparatively green and tend to set off the beauties of the Glen against the backcloth of the rugged heights. To fully appreciate the great scenery around, one should climb one or more of the quite low hills on the north side of the road from which point the whole picture becomes more vivid and real, also one can see quite clearly General Wade's road only a few hundred yards from the present motor road but a good deal higher. The story of the massacre of the inhabitants of Glencoe village by a company of soldiers under a Campbell commander is too well known to need repeating here; suffice it to say that the Macdonalds have never forgotten or forgiven although it took place as long ago as 1692. While Kingshouse is a ski-ing centre Glencoe attracts the climbers, for there are some magnificent heights, Bidean nam Bian 3,756 feet; the Three Sisters of Glencoe; the Shepherds of Etive, Buachaille Etive Mor and Buachaille Etive Beag; all are over 3,000 feet and stand out magnificently. Over 1,200 acres of this Glen and surrounding mountains belong to the National Trust for Scotland.

The scenery around the coast of North Lorn is far more varied than the inland route, high and rugged hills there are in plenty on the landward side while the coast itself is largely green and fairly fertile, particularly that tiny district known as Appin with the green island of Lismore just offshore in Loch Linnhe. From Portnacroish the road traverses the Strath of Appin to Loch Creran, the banks of which it follows for some few miles to the wild and mountain-locked Glen Creran, with a narrow road leading northwards into the hills and mountains. Southwards the road continues to follow the east bank of the Loch through the district known as Benderloch to Connel Bridge and Oban. Half-way down the east side of Loch Creran there is a side-road through Gleann Solach to Ardchattan Priory on Loch Etive. This fine old Priory is in the care of the Dept. of Environment and is worth the extra few miles quite apart from the change in scenery. A couple of miles ahead at Bonawe Quarries a ferry will take the motorist across Loch Etive to Taynuilt and on to Oban.

This district of North Lorn, some eighteen miles by twenty miles in extent, is the ideal stamping ground for the professional walker who is thoroughly accustomed to map and compass; the glens make for easier and safer walking, for the amateur or the less vigorous.

Fort William

Status: Small burgh.
How to Get There: (*By Rail.*) Good service direct from Glasgow.
(*By Road.*) Coach service from Glasgow. Also from Inverness.
Population: 4,100.
Early Closing Day: Wednesday.
Post Office: High Street.
Tourist Information Office: Cameron Square.
Places of Worship: Parish Church, Dunscanburg. A few other
denominations have places of worship.
Parking Places: There are plenty of parking places although street
parking is restricted.
Cinema: Playhouse, High Street.
Parks and Open Spaces: Town Park, Claggan.
Newspapers: Highland News (Thursday). Oban Times (Thursday).
Other Amenities: Although most of the usual resort amenities are
to hand Fort William is more concerned with the pleasures of the
countryside around.

FORT WILLIAM IS the southern gateway to the Northern Highlands
while Inverness is the northern gateway. It is rather as a first-class
shopping centre, a place to obtain the information and goods
required for expeditions farther afield than as a holiday resort, that
Fort William will be remembered. It is, however, an excellent centre
from which to explore in all directions. It was only in the seventeenth
century that Fort William had its very first beginnings when
Cromwell's troops built a small wooden fort and named it Inverlochy.
A small village grew up alongside the fort and in the early years of
the eighteenth century General Wade came north, repaired and
enlarged the fort and built the road to Inverness through the Great
Glen. Between those two events William of Orange became king and
sent troops to Inverlochy, and it was renamed Fort William after the
king. Now the fort has disappeared but the name remains. There are
no old buildings of note. Fort William is almost completely modern
although it is the centre of a land as old as any in Scotland.

The Tourist Information Office in Cameron Square is one of the
best, while the West Highland Museum and the Scottish Crafts
Exhibition should on no account be missed. From the railway station
a regular service runs to Glasgow and another to Mallaig. Both these
lines are quite remarkable in their own way and travel through
Highland country that is in every way typical. The line from Glasgow
to Fort William has been described as the finest railway achievement
in Europe. The big aluminium plant and the new papermill have gone
a long way towards providing industry other than the tourist trade,
which is, of course, immense. Ben Nevis is the one great feature that

dominates the town. Nobody should miss the trip up Glen Nevis alongside the Nevis Forest to the foot of this great mountain, which is well over 4,000 feet high, with a footpath to the summit. Some seven miles up the Glen is as far as cars can travel.

Westwards from Fort William the road goes by Loch Eil into the country that will be dealt with in the next section, while north-eastwards there is only the one road, which passes Inverlochy Castle a mile and a half north of the town. Only the outside is on view to the public but this much is well worth seeing; it is in the care of the Dept. of Environment. For the eight miles to Spean Bridge the road follows the narrow green belt between the towering height of Ben Nevis and the lovely River Lochy. Spean Bridge again is a travellers' halt but it has a very fine monument a couple of miles along the A82 from its junction with the A86. The Commando Monument is one of the finest and stands in a prominent position on a small hill next to a road junction commanding fine views especially to the south and west. The secondary road here leads across the River Lochy to Glen Loy and Loch Arkaig. Close by are some sections of General Wade's road and the ruins of High Bridge.

From Spean Bridge the A86 heads east along Glen Spean and the Braes of Lochaber.

NEWTONMORE AND KINGUSSIE

Now commences the long gentle climb along the side of Loch Moy and Loch Laggan in the shadow of Creag Meagaidh, 3,700 feet, on the north side of the road. The summit is reached at the Loch Laggan Hotel and the interesting side-road to Loch Crunachdan and beyond into the hills near the source of the River Spey right at the feet of the Monadhliath Mountains. Five or six miles farther, at Laggan, the road splits, southwards to join the A9 at Dalwhinnie, on the northernmost point of Loch Ericht. For those who really like the wildness of the heart of the Highlands there is a superb bit of scenery along a side-road from two miles east of the Loch Laggan Hotel southwards along the River Pattick to Benalder and Dalwhinnie. From Dalwhinnie the A9 closely follows the railway through the Pass of Drumochter and the glorious Glen Garry to the Wade Stone and Calvine. On the north side of the A9 the Wade road can be followed for many miles.

From Laggan to Newtonmore the Valley of the Spey softens the immediate surroundings but the high mountains are not far away, for the mighty Cairngorms are drawing nearer to the east. On a hilltop south of Laggan village is a monument to Clunie MacPherson, a great agricultural laird in the early nineteenth century, the results of whose work can be seen all along the valley towards Newtonmore. At about the half-way point to Newtonmore there are two tiny lochs under the nearby sheer sides of Creag Dhubh.

Newtonmore is a pleasant village with the fertile and wide valley of the upper Spey to set it off. The MacPherson House and Museum will be of considerable interest to many. Three miles farther along the valley is the little town of Kingussie, with one of the finest Folk Museums in Scotland; it will not matter who visits this museum they are bound to find many features of interest—the collection of agricultural implements and the Black House from Lewis are particularly fine exhibits. About a mile south of the town is the Castle of Ruthven, which was burnt by the Clans after the battle of Culloden as part of the scorched-earth policy. Here is one of the largest ski schools in Scotland and Kingussie has become one of the most popular ski centres, for in the immediate vicinity are ski slopes of every kind, for amateurs and professionals. It is barely nine miles north to Aviemore, which is barely four miles from the National Park of Glen More, which includes most of the Cairngorms as well as Cairngorm summit, which tops the 4,000 feet. Aviemore is little more than a centre from which skiers, climbers and walkers proceed into the Cairngorms and the Monadhliath mountains; it is a centre that has set itself to provide everything that the holidaymaker to these parts could require, winter sports with instructors and guides, buses and the chair-lift to within 500 feet of Cairngorm summit; accommodation to suit most pockets with caravan and camping sites. In the summer these activities are turned to summer uses with guides for parties of walkers, splendid fishing and a swimming-pool and ice-rink thrown in. Needless to say a ski patrol rescue team and first-aid station keep continuous watch. There are seven ski tows and chair-lifts to the various heights.

West of Aviemore there is a tiny loch and a Nature Reserve, while ahead the heights begin to drop and the Valley of the Spey commences to open out into the very beautiful Strath Spey. At Boat of Garten, four and a half miles from Aviemore, one begins to sense that the Highlands are behind and the fertile lands of Banff, Moray and Nairn are approaching, although it will be many miles yet before the hills are finally left behind. At Boat of Garten the road divides, the Great North Road turns left or north-eastwards towards Inverness while the A95 follows the gently widening Spey towards Dulnain Bridge, where it crosses the River Dulnain into Moray, and within three miles is in Grantown on Spey, which will be dealt with in another section.

THE CULLODEN MONUMENT
At the start of Culloden Forest the B851 leaves the A9 and within four miles joins the B9006. Turn left here, park the car in the car-park and have a quiet stroll. There is an information room run by the National Trust for Scotland who own the several acres on which are the various relics and monuments. The Memorial Cairn, the Well of the Dead, the Cumberland Stone and graves of the various Clans who

fought here, each marked by a stone engraved with the name of the Clan, make this one of the finest Scottish Memorials. Also within the grounds is the farmhouse of Leanach, thatched, and almost exactly as it was when the battle of Culloden ended so disastrously for the Scots on the 16 of April 1746.

THE GREAT GLEN AND FORT AUGUSTUS

The Great Glen, originally Glen Albyn but sometimes known as Glen Mor, is the second great geological fault across the Highlands— they both run approximately in the same direction, north-east to south-west; a straight edge if placed alongside the Great Glen will demonstrate just how straight this mighty fault is. It was along this straight and narrow gap through the mountains that General Wade built his road, and today the motor road follows almost exactly the course the General took.

At Spean Bridge the A82 turns north-east with Ben Nevis behind and over the right shoulder as the road follows closely the banks of Loch Lochy alongside considerable forest with much fine old Scotch Fir. The Caledonian Canal starts at the entrance to Loch Linnhe with eight locks known as Neptune's Staircase, and thereafter follows the Lochs and rivers of the Great Glen on its long northward journey to Inverness and the North Sea. The constructing of this great canal came about very largely as a result of the clearances of the Highlands and the subsequent emigration of much of the best blood to America and Canada; this outflow of the Highland population had reached immense proportions by 1800 and the government in London were very concerned at the possible results. Thomas Telford, the subsequently famous engineer, was sent up to investigate and report. In consequence the canal was built, employing 5,000 men during its construction, General Wade's road along the Glen was repaired and widened, while many other roads were constructed. By 1822 the canal was opened and with the help of the new roads the Highlands were opened up considerably and places that until then had been virtually unknown were brought within the realm of transport and the mail-coaches. The canal was built large enough to take the biggest traders of that day. It joins the four lochs that fill the Glen and allowed the passage of steamers and sailing craft from the Atlantic to the North Sea.

INVERGARRY AND THE SEVEN HEADS

Twelve miles from Spean Bridge is Laggan Locks and here the A82 crosses the narrow Loch Oich to the western bank by a swing-bridge. Shortly the village of Invergarry appears, with an interesting monument with seven heads which was set up by MacDonell of Glengarry and Invergarry Castle to commemorate feudal justice done; seven murderers of the Keppock family were killed, their heads washed and presented to MacDonell at Glengarry Castle.

Many of this Clan emigrated to Canada after the notorious, brutal 'clearances' of the Highlands after the rising of 1745. Invergarry Castle was built on the 'Raven's Rock' overlooking Loch Oich and the present ruin is probably the third, if not the fourth such stronghold to stand there. The existing ruin was burned down by the Duke of Cumberland in 1746. From Invergarry northwards the road follows the west bank of Loch Oich to the Bridge of Oich, where it returns to the east bank and continues, not far from the canal, to Fort Augustus. The scenery so far from Spean Bridge has been first rate, with the hills and glens on either side of the Great Glen plus a lot of natural forest and some plantations.

FORT AUGUSTUS

Fort Augustus is the second of the three forts that were constructed along the line of the Great Glen, Fort George at the narrow entrance to the Moray Firth near Inverness being the third. Apart from the lock and the six gates there is not much to see in Fort Augustus. St. Brenda's Abbey will be of great interest to those of the Roman Catholic faith but apart from these there is little to hold the motorist. Here the road splits, the A82 keeping to the west bank and the A862 crossing the canal at the extreme southern end of Loch Ness. There is a steep climb alongside the Loch and from the summit a magnificent view southwards. On either side of the Great Glen there are hundreds of square miles of sparsley populated and very wild mountain country; this is particularly so to the north and west where there are some of the greatest deer forests in Scotland.

The A862 runs through a fine stretch of country dotted with lochs and patches of forest with a number of 2,000-foot hills overshadowing the road on the east side. Twelve miles from Fort Augustus the road divides again, the A862 descending quietly passed several lochs to touch Loch Ness at the village of Dores and continue quietly to Inverness; this is the main road and a very busy one in the season. The B852 leaves the main road at this junction and, passing close to two fine waterfalls at Glenlia, skirts the banks of Loch Ness for some twelve miles before joining the A862 again at Dores. There is another road through utterly wild country along Strathnairn to the Culloden Forest and Inverness. This is, perhaps, the most scenic route, but no matter which way one travels the journey from Fort William to Inverness is one of the finest from the scenic point of view. Those interested in timber and the preservation of our naturally ancient forests will be delighted with the large number of Old Scotch Fir with the fine red bark that are to be found on either side of the Great Glen; in other parts of Scotland they appear to be almost extinct.

Dundee

Status: City. Royal Burgh.

How to Get There: (*By Rail*). Dundee is on the main Aberdeen—London line and enjoys an excellent service from both Edinburgh and Glasgow.

(*By Road.*) Local and countryside bus services are very good and through coach services to all important centres provide an excellent all-round service.

Population: 183,744.

Early Closing Day: Wednesday.

Post Office: Meadowside.

Tourist Information Centres: 21 City Square, 98 Nethergate.

Places of Worship: Parish Church, St. Mary's, Church of Scotland. Most other denominations have places of worship.

Parking Places: There are fifteen parking lots around the city centre and no difficulty should be experienced.

Cinemas: There are ten cinemas in the city. The A.B.C. Capitol, The Odeon and The Tivoli are first-run cinemas.

Theatres: Whitehall Theatre, Bellfield Street, The Dundee Repertory Theatre.

Parks and Open Spaces: Baxter Park, Caird Park, Camperdown Park, Dawson Park, Dudhope Park, Riverside Park, Stobsmuir Park, Balgay Hill, Dundee Law.

Newspapers: The Courier (daily), The Evening Telegraph (daily).

Other Amenities: Angling, athletics, swimming, boating, bowls, golf, putting, pony riding, tennis, art galleries and museums, the City Museum and Art Gallery, The Barrack Street Shipping and Industrial Museum, The Broughty Castle Museum, The Spalding Gold Museum.

FOR SOME REASON unknown the county of Angus, of which Dundee is the county town, is seldom mentioned when people talk of holidaying in Scotland. Yet it is a more than beautiful county, largely hills and glens with a rich and verdant strath around the coast and some distinguished towns to suit.

Dundee is a city built upon the labours of industry and the shipping trade over many hundreds of years; to be more exact upon the import and processing of jute, that very useful inner fibre of the jute plant which is imported from the east and, by a quick count, is used in several score of modern manufacturing processes. Dundee has always been a centre for the weaving of coarse textiles from wool, and later from cotton and the flax plant; in the 1830s jute was imported and the men of Dundee evolved a method of weaving which has resulted in the enormous jute industry of today. Shipbuilding is another old industry that stems from the days of sail and whaling in which particular industry Dundee was a famous port. During the last fifty years Dundee has grown and diversified her industries so that now few cities can have more, or a greater divergence, of industry than has Dundee.

The city itself is attractive and strikes the visitor as a modern and progressing city that has not forgotten its past. In museums it is rich, in old buildings not so rich but fortunate in the type of building remaining to reflect the past. Among these may be mentioned the following: the Old Steeple, St. Mary's Tower, is 160 feet high and one of the principal landmarks in the city. The Old Steeple is another name for the Steeple Church which is one of three under the one roof in a cruciform pattern; this must be an almost unique arrangement.

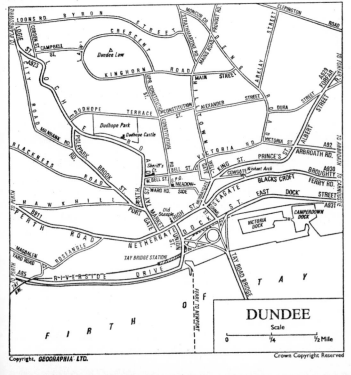

These three churches form the city churches which stand in gardens in the city centre and so give a very fine first impression. The Steeple Church is the oldest, fifteenth century, and is on the site of a twelfth-century church.

St. Paul's Cathedral is on the summit of Castlehill where in the fourteenth century Dundee Castle stood. It was designed by Sir Gilbert Scott and was built in 1853. The spire is another landmark.

Cowgate Port or Wishart Arch is the only surviving gate of Dundee's town walls; many street names commemorate the others.

Dudhope Castle is in Dudhope Park and is used as a meeting place for various sporting and cultural clubs. It was built in the thirteenth century and housed the Hereditary Constable of Dundee.

Claypotts Castle at Broughty Ferry on the eastern outskirts of Dundee was a stronghold during the Cromwellian wars and is now in the hands of the National Trust for Scotland, and is more than worth inspection.

Mains Castle in Caird Park is an early sixteenth century castle of the smaller type built rather in the style of the more elaborate peels.

A few miles north of the city at the village of Tealing is an Earth House and a Dovecote, both are under the Dept. of Environment and the Earth House is most interesting.

Perhaps the most outstanding construction in Dundee is one of the most modern. The Tay Road Bridge is completely modern in concept but delightful in every way, it fits the general picture as so many modern constructions do not.

Broughty Castle at Broughty Ferry is in the hands of the Dept. of Environment and is right alongside the old harbour in a most picturesque and outstanding situation. It was completed in 1496. Naturally as guardian of the Firth of Tay this old castle has had an historic past. Unfortunately at the present time only the outside can be viewed by the public.

Among the twenty-eight parks in the city, Camperdown certainly deserves special mention. The mansion of Camperdown was built in the 1820s, for Admiral Adam Duncan and is in the classical style with some fine ceilings and Greek pillars; it is also the home of the Spalding Golf Collection which is reputed to be one of the best. The park is certainly one of the finest monuments in Dundee, one of the most beautiful parks in Scotland. In the park is a golf-course, a field study centre, a riding stable, a children's playground and many other attractions including an aviary. The most outstanding feature is the number of different trees including many from abroad; it is said that at least one of every European tree is represented. The park is about one mile by half a mile in size.

The University with its outstanding towers is a fine building and a university of some note although it is not yet one hundred years of age.

Of those buildings mentioned the most Scottish in design is

Claypotts Castle, although the Morgan Academy is in the typically
Scottish baronial style and makes a fine picture.

Dundee spreads its docks and industries for seven miles along the
Tay, a pointer to its importance as a port; it lays at the feet of the
Sidlaw Hills which protect it from the north winds, it has a fine
coastline near at hand and the eastern highlands are not far away,
while the Carse of Gowrie to the west is immensely rich farming land.
Altogether a very nice city in a first-class situation.

THE COAST NORTH OF DUNDEE

A glance at the map will show clearly that the county of Angus
consists chiefly of two main portions. The larger is the least populated,
the foothills of the Grampians with the glens that run from north-west
to south-east in an endless succession. This area narrows towards the
northern end; between Perth and Dunkeld it is some fifteen to twenty
miles wide but at Stonehaven there is only a narrow gap between the
coast and the hills. Into the middle of this green and pleasant land
the Sidlaw Hills stretch from south-west to north-east above Dundee.
It was along the narrow gap between the Sidlaws and the foothills of
the Grampians that the Romans marched with many a suspicious look
over their shoulders, and up the dark glens in which the Picts were
no doubt hiding. The best way to explore this fascinating land will be
to travel northwards up the coast and return by the road the Romans
took.

Broughty Ferry with the harbour and castle is the first place and
right on the outskirts of Dundee; this is the nearest seaside spot to
Dundee and it boasts a long sandy beach with most of the amenities
that the folks of Dundee on a day's outing would be looking for. It is
on the western end of a long half-moon of a bay and so is a pleasant
place for holidays. A favourite walk is across Barry Sands to the two
lighthouses or to Carnoustie.

CARNOUSTIE. Population 5,650

As one might expect in a place with a reputation for golf such as
Carnoustie's this is a fine and most pleasant little town with the air
of a new planned community, with excellent bus and rail connections,
a Council that lacks nothing in making the arrangements for all to
enjoy their stay, and a sandy beach that must attract thousands in the
summer. However, Carnoustie does not cater for summer visitors alone
but rather it makes a big point of winter entertainments and really is a
gay place for those who prefer this type of holiday. For the keen
golfer of course there is no place quite like Carnoustie.

So far the road has not been particularly pleasant, for a few miles
north of Dundee it tends to be built-up but northwards from
Carnoustie it improves as it passes through the little village of
Easthaven where, in complete contrast to Carnoustie, rocks line the

shore and the inhabitants are nearly all fisherfolk. This is as far as the coast road goes as it turns towards the main road and Arbroath.

Arbroath

Status: Royal and Ancient Burgh.
How to Get There: (*By Rail.*) On the main London–Aberdeen line with fast and frequent services to Glasgow and Edinburgh.
(*By Road.*) Good bus and coach service to Aberdeen, Glasgow and Edinburgh with connections to all important centres.
Population: 21,000.
Early Closing: Day: Wednesday.
Post Office: Hill Street.
Tourist Information Office: 105 High Street.
Places of Worship: Parish Church, The Old Church, Kirk Square. Some other denominations have places of worship.
Parking Places: Ample car-parking arrangements, restricted street parking, car-parks and street parking.
Cinema: The Palace, James Street.
Parks and Open Spaces: Springfield Park, Macdonald Park, Inchcape Park, Carnegie Park, Low Common, Cricket Common, West Links, Victoria Park.
Newspapers: The Arbroath Herald (Friday), The Arbroath Guide (Friday). The Dundee Courier and Advertiser (daily).
Other Amenities: Sea angling, golf, tennis, river fishing, dancing, bowls, bathing, indoor swimming, putting.

IN THE TWENTIETH century Arbroath divides its energies between entertaining the many visitors and industry, of which fishing still takes a share. But many centuries ago Arbroath was a very small monastic town with a large and beautiful Abbey and a resident Abbot; no doubt at that time fishing was the chief industry. In this quiet little monastic town on the 6 of April 1320 there was signed the Declaration of Scottish Independence.

The remains of the Abbey, and the Abbots House which is largely complete, in locally quarried beautiful red sandstone, coupled with the Declaration of Independence, make of Arbroath a very special place.

South of the town the coast mainly consists of glorious sandy beaches but northwards is a coastline of rare attraction and beauty as the red sandstone takes over from the sandy beaches and makes of the next few miles of coast a magnificent playground of cliffs, fallen rocks and caves. Dickmont's Den and The Deil's Head are two outstanding features. One of the caves contains relics of the days when it was used by smugglers.

The harbour at Arbroath is an interesting and busy place when so many of the smaller harbours are falling into disuse. Apart from the Abbey and Abbot's House the most impressive building is the mausoleum built as a memorial to Mrs. Patrick Allan-Fraser, who died in 1873. The variety of the sculptor's work is little short of amazing. While this building may not be of importance historically it was all done by Arbroath men and is one of the finest examples of its kind.

Arbroath is a Royal and Ancient Burgh, and as a holiday town, offers pretty well all that the modern holidaymaker requires; good shops and most of the entertainments. For those interested in historical subjects the small museum near St. Vigean's Church should be visited for the fine collection of Pictish stones, sculptured in the usual Pictish manner. They no doubt date from 400 or 500 B.C., and if one remembers that the Abbey, now a ruin, did not appear until the twelfth century A.D., one gets some idea of the lapse of time since the Painted Men worked on these stones. In the Council Chambers can be seen several remarkable documents, the oldest of which dates from the prosperous days of Arbroath Abbey, from the thirteenth to the sixteenth centuries.

Montrose

Status: Royal Burgh.
How to Get There: (*By Rail*). On the main London–Aberdeen line with a fast and frequent service to Edinburgh and Glasgow.
(*By Road.*) Good bus and coach service to Edinburgh and Glasgow with connections to all important centres.
Population: 10,702.
Early Closing Day: Wednesday.
Post Office: Bridge Street.
Tourist Information: 212 High Street.
Places of Worship: Old Church, High Street.
Parking Places: Murray Lane, Western Road, The Mall, Beach Promenade, Mid Links.
Cinema: The Playhouse, John Street.
Parks and Open Spaces: Green Belt, Mid Links, West End Park, East Links.
Newspaper: Montrose Review (Thursday).
Other Amenities: All the usual holiday attractions and sports as well as a delightful coastline.

THE FIRST THING that probably strikes the visitor is the tremendous view of Montrose and surrounding district from the hilltop south of the town, as well as the spaciousness and the gardens of this Royal Burgh. Two features are particularly outstanding, the gardens with magnificent roses and the Closes, for which Montrose is rightly famed. The High Street is possibly one of the finest in Scotland while the spire known as the Steeple is another outstanding landmark. This Burgh is rich in parks, both in quality and quantity, and gardens seem to flourish extraordinarily well in Montrose. In addition Montrose is blessed with six miles of sand and sea stretching away up to St. Cyrus Nature Reserve, and with a safe yachting basin and wildfowl sanctuary, although not official, in the Montrose Basin west of the town; for this most delightful of seaside towns is almost surrounded by water, the sea and the entrance to the Basin and harbour, and the Basin itself.

The past, and the growth of this town, has been almost entirely connected with the sea, and today it is little different. Then it was sailing barques and whalers, now it is motor-ships and steamers, but the men still, to a considerable extent, go to sea; and if they do not go to sea they sail on the Basin. A couple of days spent exploring Montrose will reveal many treasures of the past, some simple and moving, some rich and almost unique.

As a modern holiday resort Montrose is first class and provides everything that one can ask for: good shops and entertainment of high calibre. Across the wide mouth of the River South Esk, which is the entrance to the harbour and the Basin, is a bridge connecting Montrose with the south shore and a number of tiny villages, as well as Lunan Bay, the ruins of Red Castle and the magnificent cliff scenery at Redhead Point at the south of Lunan Bay, and red sandstone cliffs north of Arbroath. A very delightful situation. One

The Cairngorm Mountains

Aboyne Games

Balmoral Castle

Rhynie, The Square

Rhynie, The Square

of the most remarkable features of Montrose's past is the collection of rare and ancient books in the Library, the oldest dating from 1475, a little before printing had begun elsewhere. In early June the Montrose Festival takes place; both local and imported artists perform, amateur and professional, and the variety of cultural activities is surprising and worthy of a much larger town, although the local and Scottish flavour persists right through this very excellent week. At Boddin headland, a little south of Montrose, semi-precious stones can be found and the situation is delightful.

North of Montrose the sands stretch away through the Nature Reserve of St. Cyrus to the sharp headland which marks the end of the sand and the beginning of the cliffs. This coastal Reserve is of very special note and should be visited; it contains a vast number of different sea-birds as well as the moorland types, the Curlew among them, and the little birds usually associated with meadowland. It is said that few, if any, towns have as many different species within a few miles as Montrose, and many of them can be seen in close proximity to the town itself. Seals also frequent this coast and the variety of wild flowers is quite amazing. Close to the village of St. Cyrus is the Kaim of Mathers. A medieval castle with a particularly gruesome history, it sits on a rocky outcrop nearly surrounded by the sea and certainly almost inaccessible; the ruins are very well worth a visit, if only for the outstanding situation.

There are two roads northwards from Montrose to Stonehaven—the inland road goes by Laurencekirk while the coast road passes through several interesting places. The first is the village of Johnshaven which had connections with Aberdeen Grammar School in 1262. It has an attractive little harbour and is concerned largely with fishing. The village of Gourdon is likewise an attractive village with a nice little fishing harbour.

INVERBERVIE. Population 1,000

The Royal Burgh of Inverbervie has nothing special to offer the visitor but is, nevertheless, a very pleasant base from where to explore up and down the coast and inland. The Royal Charter was granted in 1341 and was confirmed in 1595 by King James VI. The very ancient Mercat Cross is the outstanding feature while the coast, both north and south, is full of delights and interest. The builder of the famous clipper *Cutty Sark* at Dumbarton was born here. Inland around Inverbervie is some fine rambling country and the coastal walk to the rock-girt Gourdon and its busy little fishing harbour can be very rewarding. A visit should be paid to the very old Church of Kinneff about three miles north of Inverbervie, where the Honours of Scotland—the Sword, Sceptre and Crown—were buried and remained until the Restoration in 1660. This is a plain but very lovely little church on the cliff-top. Inverbervie has a first-class camping site close to the shore which here is largely shingle. There are some fine coastal views from the Todhead Lighthouse a little north of Kinneff, and between these two are the ruins of Whistleberry Castle.

Two miles before entering Stonehaven a notice at the side of a house and car park indicates that here is Dunnottar Castle, which is approached along a short footpath; the situation is, scenically, one of the finest. On a rock-girt coast out of a small bay a towering lump of sandstone rises almost sheer on three sides whilst the fourth is very steep and narrow. Up this slope a path was constructed which passes through a tunnel in the main mass of sandstone to the castle, which rises from that point to the heights above. There is a good deal of the old structure left and, apart from the situation, is well worth a visit. The whole coastline from the vantage points presents a picture of split and tumbled rock masses and is most fascinating. This extraordinary spot, including the castle, is open to the public.

Stonehaven

Status: Police Burgh.
How to Get There: (*By Rail*). Being on the main London, Edinburgh and Aberdeen line Stonehaven has a first-class rail service. (*By Road.*) Excellent coach services both north and south with bus services to all inland districts.
Population: 4,837.
Early Closing Day: Wednesday.
Post Office: Allardice Street.
Tourist Information Centre: Market Square.
Places of Worship: Dunnottar Parish Church, South Church, Fetteresso Parish Church, St. James' Episcopal Church and St. Mary's Roman Catholic Church.
Parking Places: Market Square, The Swimming Pool.
Cinema: Allardice Street.
Theatre: Amateur Dramatics are staged in the Town Hall on occasions.
Parks and Open Spaces: The Queen Elizabeth Park, Cowie Park, Mineralwell Park.
Newspaper: The Mearns Leader (Friday).
Other Amenities: Swimming, golf, bowls, tennis, angling, putting, dancing, children's competitions, sailing, boating, caravan site.

JUST BEFORE DROPPING downhill into Stonehaven the War Memorial will be noticed on a small hilltop on the coast side. It is a most unusual memorial being rather like a Greek temple, but is none the less a very fine one. Stonehaven is a rather nice resort, blending, as it does, the old with the new, and a great deal of both in the fine old red sandstone of the area. Old Stonehaven, known as Stanhyve in olden days, is roughly around the harbour, while New Stonehaven graces the southern approaches. In many ways this Burgh and County Town of Kincardineshire is a handsome spot.

In the harbour are boats and a small fishing fleet but no fish are sold here; twenty-five years ago Stonehaven was one of the busiest east coast fishing harbours. However, the yachts of the local squadron add interest and beauty to the picture; sailing is a popular pastime. At the harbour is the oldest building, the Tolbooth, dating from approximately 1600; it has been modernised but has lost none of its charm and sports on the outside a large barometer. Inside are relics of the days when local clergymen were imprisoned here by the then new sect of Presbyterianism. The fine tree-lined Market Square was at one time the scene of the weekly market, while the Market Building, built in 1827, has a 130-foot steeple which is a prominent landmark from many points of the town. The finest view of this one-time fishing village is from the A92 near the War Memorial. Like most seaside towns in Northern Scotland Stonehaven has grown and diversified her industry. Stonehaven has done it nicely with an eye open for the comfort of visitors, for whom all the usual amenities are to hand, including a heated outdoor swimming-pool.

Inland there is some fine scenery with the Valley of the Dee not far away. Northwards along the coast the scenery gets less and less interesting as one approaches Aberdeen. South of Stonehaven and very close to Dunnottar Castle is Dunnottar Kirk, which is one of the two parish churches of Stonehaven; it is more than an interesting old kirk for on this site there was a kirk in the fifth century, another in the twelfth, and after several rebuildings the present kirk was the result of reconstruction in 1903. Close to Stonehaven is the Kirton of Fetteresso, a very lovely little village with a ruined thirteenth-century church and the remains of Fetteresso Castle, dating, in its earliest parts, from the very early seventeenth century. In the same parish are the remains of a Roman Camp at Raedykes, which was joined by road with other camps at Fordoun and Normandykes. Close to the latter place is a Pictish Standing Stone with an inscription in Ogham.

Northwards from Stonehaven there are one or two places of interest before Aberdeen is reached. On a headland a mile north-east is the ruined Kirk of Cowie, and the very small remains of Cowie Castle with, below, a few cottages which are all that remain of the one-time Burgh of Cowie. The kirk is of particular importance since it is one of the very few examples of the Early English style of architecture in north-east Scotland; it was dedicated to St. Mary as long ago as 1276.

Four miles north of Stonehaven is the Seatoun of Muchalls, a popular holiday resort especially with artists. It stands on the cliff-top among coastal scenery of almost unsurpassed beauty on this

rock-bound coast. Close by on the west side of Muchalls is
Muchalls Castle, a fine example of a Scottish Laird's house of the late
seventeenth century, but is only open to the public on a few
occasions and is still occupied.

Between here and Aberdeen the scenery is not of the best and
created in the mind of Sir Walter Scott the bleak Drumthwacket Moor
of *Legend of Montrose*. For some way, however, the coastal scenery
retains its ruggedness, although the discovery of North Sea Oil is
making its impact in the area.

Aberdeen

Status: City.
How to Get There: *(By Air)*. Direct service from London, Glasgow
and Edinburgh.
(By Rail.) Main-line service to Edinburgh and London. Main-line
service to Inverness with connections to Wick and Thurso also to
Kyle of Lochalsh.
(By Road.) Good coach service south to Edinburgh and north to
Inverness. Excellent bus service to all local and inland districts.
Population: 210,000.
Early Closing Day: Wednesday or Saturday.
Post Office: Crown Street.
Tourist Information Centre: St. Nicholas' House, Broad Street,
Information Caravan, A92, and at the beach.
Places of Worship: St. Andrew's Episcopal Cathedral. Most other
denominations have places of worship.
Parking Places: Numerous and convenient. Off-street parking and
restricted street parking.
Cinemas: Odeon, Justice Mill Lane, Playhouse, Union Street,
Capitol, Union Street, Gaumont, Union Street, A.B.C., Shiprow,
Cosmo, 2 Diamond Street, Queen's Cinema, Union Street, Cinema
House, Skene Terrace.
Theatres: H.M. Theatre, Schoolhill, concerts, wrestling, shows and
exhibitions, Cowdray Hall. Mitchell Hall at Marichal College, The
Aberdeen Arts Centre, King Street.
Parks and Open Spaces: Victoria Park, Seaton Park, Hazlehead,
Duthie Park, Johnston Gardens. All told there are nine parks and
thirty-five gardens, parks and sports centres.
Newspapers: The Press and Journal (daily), The Evening Express
(daily), The People's Journal (northern edition) (Friday).
Other Amenities: Golf, swimming, gliding, skin-diving, water ski-ing,
bowls, angling, tennis, ice skating and curling, rowing and boating,
horse riding, and a host of evening entertainments as well as art
galleries and museums.

ABERDEEN, THE GRANITE CITY of nearly 200,000 inhabitants
with a recorded history going back to the twelfth century, is a big
industrial complex, a great holiday resort and the centre from which
to explore the Grampians, the River Dee and all the glorious country
that forms the backcloth to this, the greatest fishing port in Scotland.

Aberdeen's history was first recorded in the twelfth century when
a charter was granted by King David I. The charter of 1398 and the
Burgh records since that day are housed in the Town House, a record
few other cities could equal.

The view of the Mercat Cross, the Town House with its clock and
steeple and the Tolbooth with a shorter steeple make a fitting
introduction to Aberdeen, and they are right in the centre of the city.
Public executions took place outside the Tolbooth as late as 1857.

Almost next door to the Tolbooth is the Marischal College, a part
of Aberdeen University, which was founded in the early sixteenth
century on the completion of King's College, and today nearly
10,000 students study at the various colleges which form the
twentieth-century University. Marischal College is generally recognised
as the finest granite building in the world. King's College, next to
the Cathedral of St. Machar in Old Aberdeen, is the oldest school of
medicine in Great Britain and contains in its library close on 350,000
volumes.

The Mercat Cross should be viewed separately for in its own right it
is a fine piece of architecture and an ancient monument, as well as
the finest Mercat Cross in Scotland.

Provost Ross's House in Shiprow is the oldest house in Aberdeen;
it was built in 1593 and after a recent restoration is open to the public
on certain days. It is an outstanding example of the late sixteenth
century.

St. Andrew's Cathedral at the top of King Street will be of great
interest to Americans for it is the Mother Church of the Episcopal
Communion in the United States. The first American Bishop, Dr.
Samuel Seabury, was consecrated here in 1784, while the church of
St. Nicholas, with its magnificent carillon, should not be forgotten.

A little farther away off Skene Street is the Grammar School and
Byron Statue. Aberdeen has had a Grammar School since at least
1262.

Aberdeen is full of interesting buildings, both old and new; there
are so many that should be seen but which space forbids the mention
of. One, however, is the most important in the city, and this is St.
Machar's Cathedral, which was founded in 1136; the earliest part of
the present structure dates from the thirteenth century. The original
Chapel was founded during the lifetime of St. Machar in 594.
Probably the most outstanding feature is the heraldic ceiling, which
contains several rows of heraldic designs representing the kings and
princes of Europe as well as the Scottish clergy and nobility. This is a

unique ceiling in which Pope Leo X is represented, and this highlights a very surprising fact, that for several hundred years a Presbyterian congregation has worshipped under a representation of the Pope. St. Machar's is built of granite which fact no doubt gives it the militant and fortress-like appearance in spite of its small size; in addition it is beyond doubt Scottish. Among the many fine features is the west window with seven tall and narrow lights. Most of the surviving portions of St. Machar's date from the late fifteenth and early sixteenth centuries, while the most impressive feature, the great oak ceiling with the magnificent decorations, was installed in the early sixteenth century.

The situation of the Cathedral is remarkably beautiful in a small piece of parkland close to the River Don and surrounded by trees: the atmosphere is entirely academic and is heightened by the surrounding houses and gardens of the University professors. A short distance away is King's College, which is built in the form of a quadrangle of which two sides are original, from the early sixteenth century. Among the many glories of King's College is the Chapel, which contains some of the finest wood-carving in Scotland. Much

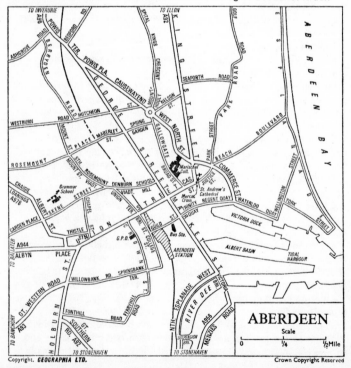

ABERDEEN

Scale

0   ¼   ½ Mile

of it dates from around 1500 and some must be unique in Scotland.

Old Aberdeen, in which are St. Machar's and King's College, is the heart of historic Aberdeen, and for many hundreds of years has been the academic centre; it has a completely different atmosphere to New Aberdeen, which is the business and tourist centre. While still in Old Aberdeen the Botanic Gardens should be visited, as should the Auld Brig o' Balgownie which, since 1320, when it was built, has been the main crossing of the River Don on the journey north. It is a single-arch bridge of close on 20 yards and below are some deep salmon pools where at the right season hundreds of salmon can be seen swimming up-river. A peculiar legend attaches to this Auld Brig, that one day it will collapse under the weight of 'a wife's ae son, and a mear's ae foal'; it is also said to have connections with Robert the Bruce. Since Aberdeen is bounded by two rivers, the Don and the Dee, it might be expected to have a number of bridges, of which the Brig o' Dee in the south of the city is extremely interesting. Built in about 1520 it has seven arches and during its reconstruction last century great care was taken to preserve the faces and retain the medieval character.

From the holidaymaker's point of view Aberdeen has one great advantage over most large cities—it has not spread its industries along the coastline but only around the harbour, which is still largely concerned with fishing and sales of fish. From Aberdeen harbour since time immemorial great fleets of fishing vessels, latterly trawlers, have gone forth to any quarter that promised good catches; for a very long while Aberdeen has been the greatest fishing port in Scotland.

The two miles of golden sand with which Aberdeen is blessed come right to the door of the city and give Aberdeen the air of any seaside resort built close to good sands and excellent bathing. There are many, many more features of interest and beauty than can be mentioned here—go forth and explore with the help of the information contained here and much that can be obtained in the city, but do not miss a visit to Rubislaw Quarry, the great man-made hole in the ground. It is 450 feet deep and out of these depths has come, for centuries past, the granite from which Aberdeen has been built; it is one of the most astounding sights.

Peterhead

Status: Burgh.
How to Get There: (*By Road*). Bus service to Aberdeen with connections to all important centres.
Population: 14,600.
Early Closing Day: Wednesday.
Post Office: Marischal Street.

Tourist Information Centre: Town Clerk's Office.
Places of Worship: Parish Church, Peterhead Old Parish.
Parking Places: Free, Broad Street, Catto Drive, Charlotte Street,
Landale Road, Station Road, Victoria Road, Windmill Street, at the
Bathing Station.
Cinema: The Playhouse, Queen Street.
Parks and Open Spaces: The Lido, South Bay, Raemoss Park,
Eden Gardens, Catto Park.
Newspaper: Buchan Observer (Tuesday).
Other Amenities: Bathing, both baths and sea, angling, bowling,
golf, putting, tennis.

AS ONE TRAVELS up the coast from Dundee the foothills of the
Grampians will have been seen to close in until at Stonehaven they
almost reach the sea. North of Stonehaven the hills retreat to allow
room for the straths of the Dee and the Don which enclose
Aberdeen in a green countryside. North of Aberdeen this carse land
continues right across the seaward corner of Buckie, whose blunt
nose extends into the North Sea. It is approximately thirty miles from
Aberdeen to Peterhead, and the road runs within a mile or two of the
coast through a countryside that varies from good farming land to
a fairly bleak and treeless windswept tract where the granite is
close to the surface. While the Dee is a granite river the Don flows
through a much kinder country, where farming is prosperous. The
Dee is therefore a very much more spectacular river especially in its
higher reaches.

   Northwards from Aberdeen the coast road runs close to the sea
through a featureless but pleasant region, with a number of villages
to Balmedie, where there is a glorious stretch of golden sand, and on
to Newburgh, where the River Ythan is an excellent salmon and sea
trout stream. Collieston has a tiny picturesque harbour and cliff-top
cottages with a fine cliff walk to Hackley Bay, where the sands appear
once more. Between Newburgh and Collieston are the Sands of
Forvie, one of the biggest areas of wind-blown sand in Scotland,
with the northern half of the sands a Nature Reserve. A little north of
Collieston is Cruden Bay and Slains Castle, which stands on a headland
and was described by Dr. Johnson as 'only a continuation of a
perpendicular rock'. This is a spectacular piece of coastline where the
action of the sea has worn away the veins of softer rock, leaving the
granite in a multiplicity of caves and fantastic shapes. Near Slains
there is one cave nearly 200 feet deep, which is known as Hell's Lum,
but at the Bullers of Buchan the sea drives into a hole with walls
100 feet high, known as the Pot of Birss Buchan. This is, perhaps, the
most fascinating of the many impressive features of this outstanding
coast. Shortly the village of Boddam with a castle ruin and three miles
farther is Peterhead.

Peterhead is essentially a fishing port although there is very much less fishing than there was twenty or thirty years ago. It is also a holiday resort with much to attract the visitor. The harbour is unusually large and includes a small beach set off by a fine wide grass verge. The War Memorial is a particularly fine one. South of Peterhead is the coast of caves, cliffs and rocks worn into fantastic shapes, while northwards, as far as the eye can see, is golden sand. Peterhead offers all the usual amenities and can be counted among the most pleasant of east coast resorts.

Fraserburgh

Status: Burgh.
How to Get There: *(By Road)*. Excellent bus and coach service from Aberdeen and Banff with connections to all important centres.
Population: 10,729.
Early Closing Day: Wednesday.
Post Office: Commerce Street.
Tourist Information Centre: Saltoun Square.
Places of Worship: Parish Church, Old Parish Church, Saltoun Square.
Parking Places: Saltoun Square, Shore Street, The Harbour, The Links, Albert Street, Finlayson Street, Castle Street, Hanover Street.
Newspaper: Fraserburgh Herald (Friday).
Other Amenities: Swimming (a good beach but swimmers are advised to watch the red flag and the buoys marking the limits of safe swimming), baths and children's paddling-pool, angling and freshwater fishing, golf, bowls, tennis, putting, dancing.

APART FROM ABERDEEN, Fraserburgh is one of the main centres of population and industry in Aberdeenshire; it is also one of the chief holiday resorts. Fishing and fish sales together form the backbone of Fraserburgh's industry as they have for many hundreds of years, for there has been a settlement here, on Kinnaird Head, since before historical records were kept and Fraserburgh became a Burgh in 1546. Today it is a town of well-laid-out streets, wider than most, with gardens and a magnificent beach which stretches for several miles south of the harbour around Fraserburgh Bay. Here are the prerequisites of a popular seaside holiday: the caravan park, the bathing pavilion, children's playground, including a miniature railway, and all the amenities.

The harbour is the largest on the east coast of Scotland apart from Aberdeen and is an exceptionally busy spot. Unlike so many fishing ports that have discarded the fishing of herring, Fraserburgh continues in the old herring tradition and during the season lands and sells

many, many tons. The Kinnaird Head Lighthouse and the Lifeboat are
both open for public inspection at certain times.

It is at Kinnaird Head that the coast of Buchan turns west towards
the Moray Firth. Two little places are worth a visit before the county
boundary is reached between Pennan Head and Troup Head. The
first, Sandhaven, is a fishing village with no fishing and the harbour
falling into ruin. It is a rather nice but sad spot that is kept clean and
tidy; in fact some of the cottages are beautifully decorated. The second,
Rosehearty, is similar to Sandhaven but quite a bit larger and with the
obvious intention of becoming a small resort. Rosehearty is a Burgh
with plenty to attract the visitor who requires peace and scenic beauty.
Immediately west of the Burgh is coastal rock scenery of a very high
order while the pier of the one-time busy harbour makes a fine fishing
stance. There is an outdoor swimming-pool, with a special one for
children, and a bowling green.

INLAND ABERDEENSHIRE

Both the A98 and the A981 head south-west from Fraserburgh
towards the distant hills and mountains, and both start rising gently
almost at once. Over the first few miles to Strichen and New Pitsligo
little of interest is encountered; however, the motorist will notice
neatly piled heaps of cut peats on the roadside and wonder whether
the farmer, for this is not a crofting countryside, uses them for fuel;
a few are used as fuel but the great majority are used in the making
of blended whisky, the fumes from peat fires adding that touch of
flavour we have all admired.

South of Strichen is New Deer and a few miles nearer Peterhead
is Old Deer, the core and centre of Buchan. Old Deer sits on the
well-wooded Ugie Water and is nicely distributed around the church,
which is eighteenth century. Nearby are the ruins of the
thirteenth-century Abbey of St. Mary, which was founded by William
Comyn. Old Deer is famous for something a great deal more ancient
than the Abbey, the Book of Deer, an MS. which is today in the
University Library at Cambridge but was written in the seventh-century
Monastery founded by St. Drostan. This is believed to have been one
of the earliest Christian institutions in the north of Scotland.

Thirteen miles west of New Deer is the interesting village of
Turriff, with a beautifully proportioned bridge across the River
Deveron, which forms the western boundary of ancient Buchan. The
village is graced with three nice red sandstone churches and close by
is Delgatie Castle, the seat of the Hay Clan. It was rebuilt by the
Hays in the early fourteenth century on earlier foundations, and has
a great deal in the way of painted and groined ceilings, pictures,
armour, etc., as well as a turnpike stair.

Some twenty-five miles south-west of Turriff is one of the most
interesting little towns in this part of Aberdeenshire. Huntly is a busy

and apparently prosperous town with the pleasantest of appearances
and an old castle to which the public are admitted by the Dept. of
Environment on certain days; this was originally Strathbogie Castle
and is virtually all fifteenth century. Here the hills are reaching upwards
and the Cairngorms are nearly in sight. The country as a whole is
well wooded and fair farming land, with the pleasant outlook
expected. Southwards through the narrow neck of this pleasant
strath leads to wilder country, Clashindarroch Forest, through which
the River Bogie and the road thread a pleasant path; side-roads lead
off into the hills. After about nine miles both the river and the road
arrive at the village of Rhynie, which is well in among the foothills.

KILDRUMMY AND GLENBUCHAT CASTLES

While there is nothing very special about Rhynie village the two
nearby castles are very special indeed. They are both in the hands of
the Dept. of Environment and are open to the public. Kildrummy is one
of the finest fortresses of the thirteenth century and even after
700 years shows the fine workmanship put into it; a great deal of it
remains much as it was built and in fine condition. The position of
Kildrummy was of prime importance at the time of erection since it
stands at the southern entrance or exit of the pass to the Moray Firth,
and a glance at the map will show this. Prior to the building of
Kildrummy there was a Norman motte and bailey about a mile
north-east of the present castle but nothing remains today; there
are, however, the remains of the ancient parish church which
stood very close to the first wooden castle; they stand in a prominent
position on a small mound where flints, implements, etc., have been
found, indicating earlier inhabitants than the Normans. Kildrummy is
nine miles south of Rhynie while Glenbuchat is a further four miles
along the A97.

Glenbuchat is, and always has been, a Gordon castle. The older
castle was farther up the beautiful Glenbuchat Glen and its site can
still be distinguished. The present Glenbuchat Castle, only very
partially a ruin, was built in 1590. Over the castle doorway is a motto
which is unfortunately no longer legible but which ran thus: 'John
Gordone   Helen Carnegie   1590   nothing on earth remains bot
faime.' The word 'faime' here has its old meaning of 'good repute'.
Both these castles are among the finest of the ruined or half-ruined
castles of this part of Scotland and the run up Glen Buchat should
not be missed. Continue past Badenyon in a circle to Strathdon.

North of Rhynie and a mile south of the junction of the A97 and
the A979 is the National Trust for Scotland property of Leith Hall,
Kennethmont. This is a very unusual house built around a central
courtyard. It dates from the middle seventeenth century and the
National Trust property includes 320 acres in which there are some
very beautiful gardens.

A shade over a mile east of Rhynie on a narrow side-road is Druminnor Castle and Museum, which dates back to the fifteenth century and is said to be haunted by a number of Gordons who were killed by the Forbes, owners of the Castle, and their hosts at the time. It is open at certain times.

Near the village of Insch, which is fifteen miles east of Rhynie on the A979, are a number of interesting ruins, including the Picardy Stone near the hamlet of Mireton, and farther along the same road, close to where it joins the A96, are more ruins, while two miles east along the A96 at Pitcaple is Pitcaple Castle, a very fine fifteenth-century building. It is open to the public at certain times, being still occupied. If the A96 is followed north-westwards for a few miles to the Glens of Foudland Skares in the lower foothills, and a side-road taken to the Wells of Ythan, the motorist will be at the source of this lovely little river which has, or had, the reputation of being one of the best pearl-fishing rivers in Scotland. Nearby is the little village of Forgue, where in the kirk will be found what is believed to be the oldest silver communion cup used in the Church of Scotland; it dates from about the middle of the sixteenth century. About a mile to two miles east of Ythan Wells, at a spot known as Glenmailen, is the most northerly point reached, for certain, by the Romans; the site of their camp can still be recognised. From this far point in the long march from Rome the prospect is of high hills to the west, while eastwards the moors slowly give way to the green lands on the coast north of Aberdeen. The reach of the River Ythan below Fyvie is particularly beautiful and well worth the detour to see it in its deep ravine below the Braes of Fetterletter and Gight, overlooked by the ruins of the Castle of Gight; this stretch, reached from a side-road off the A947 and the B9005, is one of the loveliest pieces of river scenery in the north-east of Scotland. It continues to flow through a very beautiful countryside by the villages of Methlick and Ellon to Newburgh and the sea. The Ythan is in fact the southern boundary of Buchan and probably flows through the most beautiful stretches of this variable countryside. Ellon is the proud possessor of two of the famous beaker communion cups from the Low Countries, of about the late sixteenth or early seventeenth century, the silver-work being of an extremely high calibre.

PITMEDDEN GARDENS

The National Trust for Scotland hold some sixty-five acres and a re-created seventeenth-century Great Garden at Pitmedden, about a mile north of the village, which is six miles west of Ellon. These gardens are among the finest and most expertly handled, and a tea-room and Information Centre are on the site. West of Pitmedden is the nice village of Old Meldrum, five miles south of which is Inverurie. About four miles north of Inverurie is the Maiden Stone, a very finely carved monument that must have had religious significance probably in Celtic times, for there is a Celtic cross on one side.

Ten miles south-west of Inverurie is the village of Monymusk, which has associations with that remarkable little silver and bronze box known as the Monymusk Reliquary, which is now in the Museum of Antiquities in Edinburgh. It dates from the seventh or eighth centuries and is supposed to have been associated with the movement of St. Columba's relics from Iona to Dunkeld.

This is the region of the Upper Don, a beautiful, rich countryside which was a stronghold of the Celtic Church and has much to show the enquiring visitor. Towards the east and Aberdeen the land slopes gently down to the sea, while westwards it rises to the birthplace of the Don, many miles away on the border with Banffshire under Gael Charn, 2,207 feet, in a land where only the walker may penetrate to enjoy the glories of these hills and glens, situated in one of the grandest areas of mountain and glen and which are, in fact, the north-eastern foothills of the Grampians. Almost at the source of the Don are the remains of Corgaff Castle, which is under the Dept. of Environment and open to the public.

A very lovely run around these hills is from Rhynie to Kildrummy and Glenbuchat, then on to Strathdon, Crathie and Braemar.

Between the Don and the Dee, in their upper reaches, the foothills of the Grampians intrude to separate these two rivers by as little as ten miles at their nearest. Between the two there are several places the visitor will not want to miss. Craigievar Castle is a little south of the tiny Muir of Fowlis on the A980, and is an outstanding example of the Scottish Baronial of the early seventeenth century. The magnificent plaster ceilings are, perhaps, the finest feature of a castle that is full of them. A few miles south is the village of Lumphanan, where can be seen what is probably the finest example of a Norman motte and bailey castle in existence. It is grass grown but the outlines are distinct and a little imagination will conjure up a complete picture; it is under the Dept. of Environment, who describe it as a Peel Ring. There are, of course, many other places but lack of space forbids the mention of all.

ROYAL DEESIDE

Deeside came by the prefix Royal on account of Queen Victoria's long and ardent association with the area; it is probably true to say that it was this association and patronage that put Deeside on the map. However, quite apart from any royal considerations Deeside has a most distinctive character of its own. In its upper reaches the river can be spectacular and over its whole length it is beautiful beyond most. There is no industry and little through traffic; agriculture in a small way and tourism complete the picture, with hills rising to well over 1,000 feet even within twenty miles of Aberdeen.

The castles at Braemar and Balmoral need no description here: they are magnificent and well known. Among the many great houses and castles Crathes must take pride of place. It lies three miles east of Banchory, was built in 1596 and is famed for its painted ceilings, its gardens with yew hedges dating from 1702, and the Horn of Leys, which is a token of the original gift of these lands to the Burnetts by Robert the Bruce in 1323. This property is owned by the National Trust for Scotland and it is, of course, open to the public. Seen from the garden, which is below the castle, Crathes is one of the finest castle views in Scotland and should be the subject of a special visit. Midmar, Fraser and Cluny are three other castles in the region of Deeside or easily reached from the main valley road.

OVER THE MOUNTAINS TO ANGUS

Apart from the coast road there are only three roads south from Deeside to the more populated regions of Angus far to the south. The highest of these two is the road from Braemar, which rises to over 2,000 feet at the Devil's Elbow. This is a road with tremendous mountain scenery and distant vistas from the high points and it leads the motorist down the magnificent Glenshee to Blairgowrie. The other road is the Cairn o'Mounth. Very much shorter it runs from Banchory to Montrose, and although the hills are not so high and the views not so great, nevertheless the hills have a greater intimacy and the country a more homely look. The third is the Slug Road from Banchory to Stonehaven. This is the shortest and runs for most of its length through a high valley.

Within the area of these three roads is a country wild and mountainous with a few mountains, in the west, over 3,000 feet. Into these hills from a few points side-roads and rough tracks penetrate, notably from Kirriemuir to Kirkton of Glenisla and the A9 in Glenshee; the Glen Clova road from Kirriemuir; the side-road through Tigerton from Brechin; the Glen Esk road from Edzell and a number of small side-roads that penetrate only the outer foothills. Among this glorious mass of mountains which is cut up by glens and burns only the walker will feel at home and able to revel in the magnificent scenery.

THE CITY OF BRECHIN. ROYAL AND ANCIENT BURGH

The Cairn o' Mounth road, the B974, crosses the hills from Banchory and enters the village of Fettercairn, from where roads spread out to all the nearby villages. The most westerly passes through Edzell, which is entered through a handsome stone archway. Not far from the village is Edzell Castle and gardens; the castle dates from the early sixteenth century while the garden was cultivated in 1604 and is a veritable gem.

Five miles south of Edzell is Brechin, on the River South Esk, with its remarkable cathedral which was founded in the early years of the twelfth century, although the erection of this church is generally accepted as having taken place in the thirteenth century. A great deal older than any part of the Cathedral proper is the Round Tower which is, no doubt, a relic of the ancient Celtic Church which preceded the Cathedral. There is a good deal to be seen in and around Brechin which is a very pleasant, cosy little Cathedral city.

North-eastwards from Brechin lies good farming land, lovely little villages with a well-wooded countryside dotted here and there with the ruins of one-time great houses or castles. South-west of Brechin is the tiny village of Aberlemno, with two of the finest Pictish Stones on the roadside south-west of the village and another in the churchyard; the sculptor's work on these three stones is outstanding and has weathered the storms since the eighth or ninth century.

FORFAR. Population 10,252

Although Forfar, a Royal Burgh, is fast getting industrialised it is still a pleasant town and a good shopping centre. Among the features that should be seen is Restenneth Priory, of which the tower and spire are still standing. It is on the Arbroath road and is in the hands of the Dept. of Environment. A part of this very ancient Priory is said to date from the eighth century, a relic of the Picts. At Kirriemuir, six miles north-west, is the birthplace of Sir James Barrie, in 1860. The house where Barrie was born is in the hands of the National Trust for Scotland and is open to the public.

GLAMIS CASTLE

Six miles south-west of Forfar is the home of the Queen Mother. Glamis Castle is a fitting home for Royalty but is so well known as to need no description here. The village is partly old and partly new, the castle is all it is reputed to be, a fine example, partly of medieval and largely of early eighteenth-century castle building. To many the most attractive feature of Glamis will be very fine Folk Museum which has on show so many of the tiny and almost unimportant things that, not so very long ago, made up the everyday life of the folks of these parts. Two of the most fascinating exhibits are two rooms, one a simple cottage interior with box-beds of the Victorian age, the other a more sophisticated and socially better-class room of the same period. Perhaps the narrow tree-lined lane past the museum to the church is the best part of Glamis. In few places are trees so magnificent as in Angus, and this is noticeable all over the county and in many parts of Aberdeenshire.

On the road westwards from Glamis to Meigle the tiny village of Eassie will be passed and here in the churchyard is another of the finely carved Pictish stone crosses for which the area is famous; more, including a museum of Pictish Stones, many of them in remarkable condition, are to be found at nearby Meigle in Perthshire.

Section 5

Banffshire Moray and Nairn

Nairn

Status: Royal Burgh.
How to Get There: *(By Rail)*. On the main line from Aberdeen to Inverness Nairn has a good service of trains from both places.
(By Road.) A good coach and bus service to both Aberdeen and Inverness with a service to the surrounding areas.
Population: 5,330.
Early Closing Day: Wednesday.
Post Office: Cawdor Street.
Tourist Information Centre: King Street.
Places of Worship: Parish Church, The Old Parish Church. Several other denominations have places of worship.
Parking Places: Free parking at High Street (opposite High Church), Millbank Street, St. Ninian Road, King Street car park.
Cinema and Bingo. Regal, Leopold Street.
Parks and Open Spaces: Viewfield House with extrances from King Street, Glebe Road and Viewfield Street. The riverside on both banks of the river connected by two foot-bridges.
Newspaper: Nairnshire Telegraph (Tuesday).
Other Amenities: The West Beach, the East Beach, putting, golf, tennis, bowls, angling, swimming.

THE COUNTIES OF NAIRN and Moray have been called the Garden of Scotland, and there is some truth in this. The reason is that the coastal regions, from ten to fifteen miles wide, are protected from the worst of the north winds by the counties of Sutherland and Caithness, while the Highlands protect the western and southern flanks. To the east the foothills of the Highlands extend almost to the coast at Buckie, giving protection from the east. This area of protected land is fertile and well farmed, and is one of the driest regions in Great Britain, getting more than its share of sunshine.

Leaving Inverness the first place of interest along the coast is Fort George. The narrow strip of land along the coast from Inverness to Fort George is known as Drummossie Muir, and apart from its agricultural value is of little account; it is in Inverness county.

Highland cattle

Inverness Castle

Brig O'Dee, near Braemar

Brig O'Dee, near Braemar

Glenfinnan Monument

FORT GEORGE

This remarkable fort was built in the first place in 1726 by General Wade but was blown up and destroyed by the Jacobites in 1746. In the very next year the new, and present, fort was commenced on the extreme point of the peninsula. It is protected on three sides by the waters of the Moray Firth and on the fourth by a moat or ditch. It is without doubt an outstanding example of eighteenth-century military architecture and has been occupied as barracks ever since. This is worth an afternoon of anybody's time.

Kilravock Castle in the lovely well-timbered Vale of Nairn is a Christian Guest House and restaurant. Three miles away on the opposite side of the River Nairn is the village of Cawdor in one of the most beautiful situations. Cawdor Castle, with drawbridge, portcullis and dungeon and under a canopy of trees alongside a nameless burn, is a fine example of the fifteenth- and sixteenth-century castles. A good view can be had from the Clunas road for it is still occupied and is not open to the public. The village alone is well worth some miles of travelling.

South of Cawdor a few side-roads run around the base of the hills but half of the county is composed of mountains rising to over 1,000 feet and increasing in height as they approach the Spey Valley. Only one road crosses this magnificent piece of country, the B9007 from the A939 south of Nairn to the A938 nine miles west of Grantown on Spey.

Dunstaffnage Castle near Oban

The Royal Burgh of Nairn is a holiday resort of the nicest class with a predominance of good weather and golden sands. All the amenities are here including a large well-equipped caravan site. The town itself is a good shopping centre and a pleasant place to sojourn in. Once an important fishing centre, Nairn has, in common with so many smaller ports, declined in this respect but remains the great agricultural centre it has always been. In the country immediately surrounding the town there are many delightful places to visit. Two miles east of the town is Auldearn, where the National Trust for Scotland have the Boath Doocot or dovecote, which is on the site of an ancient castle. It was built in the seventeenth century soon after the Battle of Auldearn; the battle plan is also on display. Nine miles south-east of Nairn, just before the junction of the A939 and the B9007, is the Ardclach Bell Tower under the Dept. of Environment. Nairn owes its position and importance to the river, for here has always been a small port, a river crossing for coastwise travellers and the lovely Valley of Nairn to facilitate travel inland. Nairn, from the coast inland for some ten miles, or more, is one of the most heavily wooded areas and this adds considerably to the natural beauties.

Elgin

Status: City and Royal Burgh.
How to Get There: (*By Rail*). On the main line from Aberdeen to Inverness, has a good service of trains from both places.
(*By Road*.) A good coach and bus service to both Aberdeen and Inverness with a service to the surrounding areas.
Population: 17,050.
Early Closing Day: Wednesday.
Post Office: High Street.
Tourist Information Centre: The Plainstones.
Places of Worship: Church of Scotland, St. Giles. Several other denominations have places of worship.
Parking Places: Murdoch's Wynd, North Street, Lossie Green, Greyfriars Street, Abbey Street, North College Street, Northfield Terrace, North Guildry Street, Reidhaven Street.
Cinema: The Playhouse Cinema, High Street.
Theatre: None, but the Town Hall stages theatrical performances from time to time.
Parks and Open Spaces: The Cooper Park, Millbuies Estate with two lochs and woodlands.
Newspaper: The Northern Scot (Saturday).
Other Amenities: Swimming at several seaside resorts within six miles, bowls, tennis, putting, swimming-baths, dancing, fishing, angling.

CULBIN FOREST

BETWEEN NAIRN AND ELGIN there are miles of sand along the coast, Culbin Forest and Findhorn Bay, on the eastern point of which is the village of Findhorn, where water ski-ing, bathing and salmon fishing are popular. Four miles before entering Forres on the A96 is the Castle of Brodie which dates from the fourteenth or fifteenth century.

Culbin Forest deserves a word for here the Forestry Commission have planted a very large area of wind-blown sand and reclaimed from dereliction many square miles of coastline. Until about 1650 this piece of country was a rich farming area where corn was grown, then the sands from the west started to blow and in due time it became an absolute desert and remained so until the forest was planted about twenty-five years ago.

Inland the B9010 skirts the hills while a side-road runs right through them to the Grantown–Charlestown road along the Spey Valley. There is a secondary road which follows the Spey between these two points; it has less traffic and is altogether the more pleasant.

FORRES

Forres town is a pleasant little place and a resort distinguished by St. Laurence's Church, the Sueno's Stone, a remarkable example of Pictish art, and the very beautiful country around in which the following places will be visited by lovers of natural beauty. The River Findhorn, which flows southwards from Forres for fifty or sixty miles and is close to the road for much of this distance, besides being heavily wooded flows through some fine geological formations of granite and old red sandstone—an exceptionally beautiful river. Close to the junction of the A940 and the B9007 Randolph's Leap is an outstanding spot in a turbulent and picturesque part of the river close to its confluence with the Divie.

North-east of Forres is the village of Kinloss, with the remains of Kinloss Abbey of date 1150 and still a very beautiful ruin. While the A96 drives straight on to Elgin the secondary roads which follow close to the coast are the more interesting, and a number of villages are passed through of which Burghead is the most interesting. It has a customs post, timber imports, a boys' sea school, and a deep and fascinating well that may have been Roman but is more likely an early Christian relic. Several Pictish Stones have been found here.

From Burghead to Elgin one can nicely take in Duffus Castle, which is under the Dept. of Environment, and St. Peter's Kirk and Parish Cross in the same village.

THE CITY OF ELGIN

From many points of view Elgin is the most beautiful place in the north of Scotland. The Cathedral when in its prime of life must have

been just as fine, for today its ruins retain a glory and a beauty
that few other ruins do. The city itself shows the hand of great care
and in addition the immediate surroundings have been treated by
nature with the same loving care. The River Lossie, the Glen of
Rothes, Sheriffmill, Ladyhill and Cooper Park all show the same hand
of care whether nature's or man's. The Cathedral came to life in the
thirteenth century, a period when perfection in architecture was the
prime consideration. It suffered many trials and was partially destroyed
on several occasions but the remains today are almost beyond
compare and were described by Professor Hannah as the most
satisfactory church that ever rose in Scotland. The sunsets that can
be seen across the Moray Firth should not be forgotten; in few places
are they as colourful and glorious.

LOSSIEMOUTH

Six miles north of Elgin is Lossiemouth. Still a great fishing village
and the birthplace of Ramsay MacDonald, this fishing village has
a lot to show the visitor. West of the village the lighthouse and caves
provide the venue for a pleasant walk, while eastwards the ample
space of Spey Bay and Lossie Forest provide another enjoyable walk
while the busy fishing harbour can be relied upon to provide interest.

THE SPEY VALLEY

Thirteen miles south of Elgin the motorist comes to Craigellachie in
the Spey Valley, and it is by this road that one should journey to
Elgin, for then that lovely city is first seen from the high ground. From
this pleasant little village the Spey can be followed northwards to the
planned town of Rothes, which came to life in 1766 as a crofting
township and was created a Burgh in 1844, and along the Glen of
Rothes to Elgin. Or south-westwards to Charlestown of Aberlour and
right along the Strath Spey to Grantown on Spey, which is but a
short run to Aviemore and the Cairngorms. The Spey flows through
the heart of the hills and presents some of the grandest scenery.
Grantown is another planned town which was born in the same year
as Rothes; it is well equipped for the skier and the mountaineer and
in addition has a variety of most delightful walks of a gentle nature.
It is a first-rate holiday centre. North and south of the Spey is some
wild hill country that will make the walker feel at home; it is the
type of country where map and compass are essential.

Some four miles south of Craigellachie is the small town of
Dufftown. The home of Grants Whisky and two old castles, it is well
worth a visit. Balvenie Castle is in the hands of the Dept. of
Environment and is open to the public; Auchindoun Castle, three
miles south of Dufftown, is also under the Dept. of Environment but
is not yet open to the public. Northwards through Keith and
Fochabers takes the motorist into Banffshire.

Banff

Status: Royal Burgh.
How to Get There: *(By Rail).* The nearest railway station is
fifteen miles away at Keith, where some trains from Inverness and
Aberdeen stop.
(By Road.) Good bus and coach service from both Inverness and
Aberdeen.
Population: 3,492.
Early Closing Day: Wednesday.
Post Office: Carmelite Street.
Tourist Information Centre: Collie Lodge.
Places of Worship: Parish Church, St. Mary's. One or two other
denominations have places of worship.
Parking Places: Collie Lodge car park, Carmelite Street car park.
Parks and Open Spaces: Duff House Grounds, Banff Links and
Deveronside.
Newspaper: Banff Journal (Tuesday).
Other Amenities: Bowls, tennis, golf, open air swimming pool,
sea swimming, glorious sands, fine rock scenery.

THE COUNTY OF BANFFSHIRE is one of the most variable, in types
of countryside, in Scotland. It stretches in a narrow very uneven belt
from the sea between the Rivers Spey and Deveron to the Cairngorms.
Its neighbours on either hand are Aberdeenshire and Morayshire and
Inverness. At the northern end, the sea coast, there is a belt of rich
agricultural land gradually increasing in height to its final magnificent
altitude of well over 3,000 feet in the Cairngorms. Very roughly the
Spey and the Deveron form the eastern and western boundaries.

The run along the coast from Fochabers—one has to cross the
Spey at this little planned town of about 150 years of age—can be
very rewarding. Portgordon is very nearly dead although it was at one
time an important port and the home town of the Gordons, whose
castle still remains, and is still occupied, close to Fochabers. The
castle is not open to the public but they are permitted to use a small
part of the gardens and the loch; there is a footpath from the village
as well as a road a mile north of Fochabers that lead to the castle.

Buckie is approached by the A98, which runs through Speymouth
Forest. It is a large and busy fishing port and the largest town in
Banffshire as well as being fairly modern. The harbour and main
shopping area are on a lower level to the residential district. It
is a very pleasant resort that can offer most of the amenities
the modern holidaymaker requires, swimming and golf being
well represented.

The two little villages of Findochty and Portnockie are of no
great importance but to the visitor they are well worth viewing for

their cleanliness and colourful decorations; the inhabitants have a reputation as house-owners and have continued in competition for honour of being the cleanest townships in Scotland. Much of the coastline is extremely spectacular.

The Royal Burgh of Cullen is another of the planned towns for which this corner of Scotland should be famous. The fishing port remains a little apart from the modern resort and the whole is conveniently situated at the eastern end of a fine bay with cliffs enclosing a beach of golden sand. Like Buckie it offers the visitor all that he can ask for and is a most pleasant resort. Next comes the old-world village of Sandend, with a lovely beach and the old port of Portsoy, which shows quite clearly by its buildings, etc., that it was built upon overseas trade rather than fishing. This is a very lovely old village with the smell of the days of sail about it, a tiny harbour with a few salmon boats and some old houses that are being lovingly reconstructed.

The very individualistic village of Whitehills still retains a goodly share of its old importance as a fishing port, sports a good hotel and is pleased to see visitors; here the coast is comparatively flat, while at Banff, three miles west across Boyndie Bay, the land slopes fairly steeply to the sea at Banff Bay.

Banff itself is an unusual and attractive town with some attractive eighteenth-century houses and a small harbour which was considerably silted up when the River Deveron changed course; in consequence of this and other causes there is little fishing from Banff. For the holidaymaker the outstanding features will be the spacious beaches of golden sand, the magnificent rock scenery, especially to the east, and the very picturesque walks along the River Deveron.

Among the most important of the older buildings are the Town House, of 1798. with an unusually massive tower, the Mercat Cross of the sixteenth or seventeenth century, Duff House and Banff Castle. Duff House, of 1720, with the very extensive grounds, is the property of the National Trust for Scotland; a walk through these beautiful grounds and the woods to the Bridge of Alvah is quite an exceptional one in many ways. Banff Castle, built in 1750, is more of a mansion than a castle, and a fine specimen of the eighteenth century it is. It is now a Community Centre with a café, etc., while the grounds contain a children's playground, putting green and other amenities. From the castle there is a truly magnificent view of the Deveron Valley and the Hill o' Doune.

Macduff is purely an industrial port and boat-building centre, with a considerable amount of fishing. East of Macduff, at the Howe of Tarlair, there is a fine swimming-pool with children's facilities, café, etc., as well as a large car-park. The two places, Banff and Macduff together, make a very fine holiday resort.

Eight miles east of Banff along the coast are the two villages of

Gardenstown and Crovie, nestling at the foot of the cliffs, for the coastline is a magnificent array of broken rock around to Troup Head and the county boundary, with the accompanying bird life. The ruins of St. John's Chapel, built nearly 1,000 years ago, bear witness to the great age of the settlement. Today these are two nice, pleasant villages that welcome the traveller. Between Troup Head and Rosehearty in Aberdeenshire there is some of the finest coast scenery and many attractive walks.

For some twelve miles inland from the coast there is a fine agricultural district with many roads. Four miles south of Cullen is the Old Kirk of Deskford, under the Dept. of Environment, which is worth a visit by those interested in old architecture. Ten miles south of Banff is Aberchirder and Kinnairdy Castle. As the county narrows to a very few miles across the Strath of Islay so the roads veer off into Aberdeenshire or Moray, and only one road passes through Keith and continues south-west to Dufftown and Tomintoul, which is the last village in Banffshire, for south of Tomintoul is some of the wildest hill country leading into the Cairngorms.

The last twelve miles of the Spey Valley to the coast is a lovely district and in some ways reminiscent of Tweedsdale. Keith, in the Strath of Islay, is sometimes said to be the county town on account of its industries, age and cultural activities. It is certainly an individualistic sort of town that obviously has its own ideas and sticks to them. The A920 traverses some first-class scenery on its journey along Strath Islay to Dufftown. All the way the altitude increases and the surrounding hills get higher and more picturesque. Dufftown is famous for its whisky distilleries and the energy its inhabitants put into the task of welcoming visitors; but it is the country around that is the chief attraction. Nearby ruins of Balvenie Castle are sufficient to make a very interesting study of this somewhat unusual type of castle, which is under the Dept. of Environment.

Five miles west of Dufftown is Charlestown of Aberlour, in Strath Spey; thirteen miles east is Huntly in Aberdeenshire and on this road there is more fine mountain scenery; but the best of this type of scenery is to be had on the B9009 to the very high hill village of Tomintoul, which has a spaciousness and an atmosphere of the hills and woodlands that make it a most delightful place to stay in. From Tomintoul the A939 goes south-east to Crathie or north-west to Grantown on Spey. There is a side-road, the B9136, which travels through some champion scenery along Strath Avon to the Bridge of Avon and Marypark, which is in the Spey Valley and just east of the boundary with Moray. Southwards from Tomintoul only the walker may penetrate the mountains and glens, the burns and finally the Cairngorms.

Section 6 The Highlands north of the Great Glen

Inverness

Status: Royal Burgh.
How to Get There: (*By Rail*). Through trains to Aberdeen, Edinburgh and London. Also services to Kyle of Lochalsh, Wick and Thurso.
(*By Road*). Through coach services in summer to Edinburgh, Glasgow and London. Bus and coach connections to all parts of Scotland.
Population: 32,058.
Early Closing Day: Wednesday.
Post Office: Queensgate.
Tourist Information Centre: 23 Church Street.
Places of Worship: St. Andrew's Cathedral, Episcopal, Parish Church, Old High Church.
Parking Places: Farraline Park, Academy Street, Eastgate, Castle Street, Bank Street, Ness Walk, Milburn Road, Ardconnel Street.
Cinema: La Scala, Academy Street.
Parks and Open Spaces: Bught Park, Bellfield Park, Fraser Park.
Newspapers: Highland News (Thursday), Inverness Courier (Tuesday and Friday), Football Times (Saturday Evening).
Other Amenities: Golf, putting, tennis, bowls, fishing, swimming, ski-ing, skating, curling, horse riding, pipe and drum bands, Scottish and Highland dancing at Ness Islands and Northern Meeting Park.

THE CITY AND Royal Burgh of Inverness has always been called the Gateway to the Highlands in the same way that Perth is the southern gateway. The traveller up the Great North Road, if he stops on the summit of Drummossie Hill on the southern approaches to the city, will realise immediately why this is so and will enjoy for five short minutes one of the experiences that make the Highlands stand out in the memory for years to come. Inverness is a fine and friendly city but can offer nothing to equal the view from the southern gateway to the Northern Highlands.

To the east the Moray Firth and coastline, to the south-west Loch

Ness with the outstanding Mealfuarvonie standing guard, while to the north and north-west range upon range of mountains dominated by the massive Ben Wyvis still a good twenty miles away. Down below, almost spanning the narrows between the Beauly Firth and the Moray Firth, Inverness sits as guardian of the road that for centuries has been the only entrance to the wild and sparsley populated territory of north and north-west Scotland. Not to stop on Drummossie and let this view sink in is to miss the experience that sums up the whole of the Highlands.

The most dominating building in Inverness is the castle on Castle Hill, and it is a little disappointing to find that this massive building is quite modern and the Sheriff's Court; but Inverness is not over-concerned with the past, it is the present and the future that the people of Inverness have always had to contend with. However, this is the hill upon which have stood for hundreds of years the Royal Castles of Inverness. Life has been established at Inverness since

Pictish times. St. Columba called here, and King William the Lion fortified the city in 1180 when the first stone castle was probably built. As long ago as the fifteenth century there was an oak bridge across the River Ness that was then termed ancient, but in the seventeenth century this was replaced with a stone bridge which had a small cell in one of the arches for violent prisoners; later this was used for violent mental patients. Cromwell's troops built a citadel which was later pulled down to supply the stone for the bridge and Dunbar's Hospital, which is still standing. General Wade was here during the eighteenth century, as was Prince Charles the Jacobite; the Highland Railway came in 1855 and modern Inverness began to take shape.

Among the most interesting buildings are the Town House of last century, majestically Scottish; the Steeple of 1791, at one time the jail; Cromwell's Clock Tower, the last of the Citadel, built in 1652; Dunbar's Hospital of 1688; Tomnahurich cemetery, 220 feet above the city and said to be the most beautiful cemetery in Scotland; St. Andrew's Cathedral of 1866, a very fine but modern Cathedral built before the ultra-modern school had come to life and so retaining the feeling and atmosphere of a church. Near Culloden Battlefield, mentioned in Section 3, are the Cairns of Clava dating from the Bronze Age and constituting some of the most important Bronze Age finds in the country. The Public Library, Museum and Art Gallery in Castle Wynd contains a fine collection of Jacobite and Highland relics covering many centuries, while the Highland Craft and Information Centre at Abertarff House and at Culloden are a mine of information on these subjects. As a holiday resort and centre from which to explore the Highlands Inverness can hardly be beaten.

THE BLACK ISLE

Those motorists headed for the west coast will take the road along the east or west bank of Loch Ness, while those headed north will want to see the Black Isle before taking the long road to Thurso. The Great North Road joins the shore line of Beauly Firth as soon as it leaves Inverness with grand views of the hills as the visitor approaches Beauly, a nice village with the remains of Beauly Priory in red and grey sandstone and under the Dept. of Environment. Alternatively the car and passenger ferry can be taken from South to North Kessock and the Black Isle.

At the Muir of Ord, where there is an Information Centre, golf, and pony-trekking, etc., the motorist should turn right for the north coast of the Beauly Firth from the most southerly point of which Inverness can be clearly seen. Avoch, pronounced Augh, is a pleasant little fishing village where all the boats fish the west coast, there being a dearth of herring on the east coast.

FORTROSE AND ROSEMARKIE

These two small seaside towns together form a Royal Burgh with the ruins of Fortrose Cathedral as the outstanding architectural feature. The other feature of note is the view of Fort George from Chanonry Point or Ness, which spit of land separates the two halves of the Burgh. North of Rosemarkie the fine sandy beach gives way to towering cliffs and many caves. The road to the Fairy Glen should not be missed. At Fortrose the Cathedral and remains of the associated buildings should be seen.

CROMARTY AND CROMARTY FIRTH

The little town of Cromarty sits guardian over the entrance to one of the finest natural harbours, The Firth of Cromarty, which, with its narrow and easily defended entrance must always have been of importance to a seafaring nation. Across this narrow neck there has been a ferry for many hundreds of years. In Cromarty is the birthplace, a thatched cottage, of Hugh Miller, born 1802, who became an eminent geologist, editor and writer; it is under the National Trust for Scotland. The Mercat Cross dates from the sixteenth century and the Town House only from the eighteenth, but a bell in the dome of the Town House has an inscription and the date 1571. Although the bulk of the coastline east and west of Cromarty is of rock formations there are sandy beaches on both sides of this pleasant little town, with some fine distant views of the hills across the Firth.

The Black Isle is undoubtedly a pleasant place for a holiday but it does not have the magnificent scenery of its neighbours. The Isle is largely rich agricultural land and forest as well as being fairly flat. The run from Cromarty to Cononbridge is not very interesting but the coast of the Black Isle, as a whole, is probably the most scenic part of the Isle.

DINGWALL. Population 3,192

The Royal Burgh of Dingwall owes its origin to its position at the head of the Cromarty Firth and the cross-roads of the Northern Highlands, for here, if one wants a main road, the choice must be made, north to Thurso or west to Ullapool; there are one or two side-roads that are worth exploring, particularly the one from Marybank on the A832, which runs through Strathconon and into some very high country to finish at the western end of Beannacharain. Another one leaves the A832 three miles prior to reaching Achnasheen, and travels along Loch Fannich right among the highest hills.

There are two main roads west from Dingwall; they run together as far as Garstan, where the A832 strikes west for Achnasheen and Wester Ross and Cromarty. The A835 strikes north-west for Ullapool. Both roads take the motorist through some of the most scenic country in the Highlands but both land in country that is truly magnificent, much of it beyond description. The well-known Falls of Rogie are close to the A832, some three miles beyond Contin; there are, of course, many very beautiful waterfalls and so many places of great beauty but only a few can be mentioned here. In Dingwall the Seaforth Memorial should be seen; it is original and most unusual.

The run along the coast road which follows the northern shore of the Cromarty Firth is a pleasant run to Evanton, where a detour should be made to visit the great gorge known as the Black Rock of Novar, which is nearly one and a half miles long and of great depth. The village of Alness is separated into two portions by the River Alness and is a pleasant little spot to stop over. Invergordon is almost entirely industrial in character but provides many of the things that most resorts of more prominence deem necessary; Highland Games, fishing, golf, sea swimming and yachting are but a few. The surrounding countryside can offer the visitor some grand motor runs or first-class walking.

The run from Invergordon to Tarbat Ness is well rewarded if one is interested in castle and other ruins, in bird life or in a quiet, peaceful rest. The finest road, from the scenery point of view, is the A836, which leaves the A9 a little south of Alness and traverses some high country with tremendous views of the two Firths of Cromarty and Dornoch. At the River Oykel the motorist will cross into Bonar Bridge and the County of Sutherland; had he, however, taken the A9 he would have passed through the ancient and charming little town of Tain, which is a Royal Burgh and was once the capital of Ross.

Alongside the road from Bonar Bridge to Dornoch there are two sets of chambered cairns which are worth seeing, and a little south of the road is Creich Dun, a vitrified fort with a fine view over the Firth.

Dornoch

Status: Royal Burgh. City.
How to Get There: (*By Rail*). Bonar Bridge, thirteen miles away, is the rail-head for those travelling from the south, Golspie for those travelling from the north. A bus service connects with Dornoch.
(*By Road.*) Good bus service from Inverness with connections from Edinburgh, Glasgow and London.
Population: 993.
Early Closing Day: Thursday.
Post Office: The Square.
Tourist Information Centre: The Square.

Places of Worship: Parish Church, The Cathedral Church of Dornoch dedicated to St. Barr. A few other denominations have places of worship.
Parking Places: Free. The Square, High Street.
Newspaper: The Northern Times (Friday).
Other Amenities: Golf, swimming, sailing, angling, walking, tennis.

THE QUITE REMARKABLY nice City and Royal Burgh of Dornoch sits on the small peninsula of land that nearly cuts off the Firth of Dornoch before it gets started. Dornoch Cathedral dates from the thirteenth century and in spite of being largely destroyed in 1570 it has continued as the Parish Church of Dornoch for the past 400 years. This fine little Cathedral should not be missed. The Castle of Dornoch is now the Sheriff's Court and an hotel. The streets are wide and clean and the atmosphere is quiet and friendly, while many of the older houses have been preserved. Most sports are represented while the golden sands make swimming a delight; there are many miles of these sands.

The most picturesque road northwards is the narrow one near the sands which passes close to the ruins of Skelbo Castle, with a view of Loch Fleet. This road joins the A9 just before passing over The Mound, which is the causeway across Loch Fleet built by the Duke of Sutherland in 1811. The Loch is famous during the season of migration for its wildfowl.

Three miles east of Golspie the road crosses the railway. On the south side of the road immediately before crossing the bridge there is a pull-in and a fair example of the broch, which dates from pre-history; there are not many this side of the Orkneys so this one should be seen; it is the oldest stone dwelling known. Dunrobin Castle, which attracts the attention, is a boys' school. The villages of Brora and Helmsdale are not of particular note though very pleasant places, but the road which follows the coast for many miles to the summit and the boundary with Caithness is graced with some of the finest coastal views on a largely rock-girt coast culminating in the magnificent panorama from the Ord of Caithness at the boundary. At Helmsdale the A897 strikes away north through the Strath of Kildonan and some of the loneliest country.

CAITHNESS, THE LAND OF CROFTERS
Caithness is very different from other Highland counties; it is in fact a high plain, the southern end being mostly peat, facing the sea with a front of great cliffs broken by sandy beaches. Many of these cliffs are the old red sandstone and very picturesque. A hundred years ago, even fifty, this was crofting country over the southern half of the county and there are quite a few of the old thatched crofters'

cottages left; one or two are still occupied but most are derelict. Except in a few places crofting is a thing of the past.

Dunbeath is a beautiful village with a lovely harbour and glen, plus a waterfall and a castle ruin. The views from the north of Dunbeath of Morven and other high hills is superlative; Morven is of great account to walkers. The village of Latheron and Latheronwheel harbour are picturesque in the extreme; the church lies in a hollow by the sea while the bell tower is on a hill-top, so that the sound of the bell will carry farther. Dunbeath and Latheron are two places that suffered badly during the Clearances and the walker in the glens will find the tragic remains of the cottages. At Latheron the A895 leaves the A9 and heads straight north over splendid moorland scenery to Thurso.

The next harbour is Lybster and like all the others on this coast it is a long way below the main road. The coast is largely towering cliffs and tiny rock-girt coves. North of Lybster on the left side of the main road is the Hill o' Many Stanes, under the Dept. of Environment. It consists of about 200 stones set in twenty-two parallel rows, and dates from 1000 to 2000 B.C. In the tiny Bay of Whaligoe there are 365 steps down to the harbour but every one is well worth while.

Wick

Status: Royal Burgh.
How to Get There: (*By Air*). From Wick Airport. Weekday services to and from Inverness, Aberdeen, Glasgow, Edinburgh and London. Service to the Orkneys and Shetlands.
(*By Rail.*) Through trains to Inverness, Aberdeen, Edinburgh and London. Connections at Inverness for Kyle of Lochalsh.
(*By Road.*) During summer through bus services to Edinburgh and Glasgow. Excellent local services including Aberdeen and Inverness with connections to the whole of Scotland.
Population: 7,385.
Early Closing Day: Wednesday.
Post Office: Market Square.
Tourist Information Centre: Whitechapel Road (off High Street).
Places of Worship: Parish Church, Wick Old Parish Church, Church of Scotland. Several other denominations have places of worship.
Parking Places: Riverside car park, Camps car park, River Street car park, Tolbooth Lane car park, Louisburgh Street car park.
Cinema: The Pavilion Cinema, High Street.
Parks and Open Spaces: Bignold Park, King George V Park, both have children's playgrounds.
Newspaper: John o'Groats Journal (Friday).

Other Amenities: Fishing, tennis, bowls, golf, swimming, rock climbing, land yachting, walking.

A MILE EAST of Lybster a narrow side-road runs north to the Watten, on the Wick–Thurso road, and passes, about five miles north of Lybster, the Grey Cairns of Camster, a prehistoric monument, in the charge of the Dept. of Environment. The Royal Burgh of Wick is a pleasant resort with an airport, the main railway line from London, the Great North Road and a coastline that is difficult to beat for rugged beauty. The surrounding countryside is most un-Highland, no hills of any note, but there are many fine walks with places of interest or beauty at the end.

Just south of the town is the old Castle of Wick, while Wick Bay, on either side of which the town is built, holds all the usual holiday attractions, including the harbour, which is still a busy fishing port. North Head is the first point north of Wick where the walker and picnicker can enjoy the gigantic rocks and remarkable scenery; Noss Head with the lighthouse is the next and from here it is possible to see the cliffs of the Orkneys. A couple of miles west of Noss Head are two castle ruins that, combined with the cliff-side walk, make a nice objective. Their names are Sinclair and Girnigoe, and they are on the south of Sinclairs' Bay. West of these two castles is Ackergill Tower. Some 500 years old, it commands a fine view.

South of Wick a fine walk takes in South Head, the Grey Bools, a completely unexplained geological formation, the Old Man of Wick and the Brig o' Trams. The coastal scenery is superb.

The Stacks of Duncansby

The road from Wick to John o' Groats is not very interesting but on the road near the hamlet of Kiess are two castle ruins, both belonging to the Sinclairs. Close by are two Pictish underground dwellings marked by standing stones. Duncansby Head, beyond the famous house of the Dutchman, John o' Groats, is a magnificent headland with wonderful views which include the nearby Island of Stroma. The nearby church where John o' Groats was buried is well worth a visit.

A little to the west is Gills Bay, the Man of Mey and St. John's Point, with the Castle of Mey, belonging to the Queen Mother, a little farther west again. Dunnet Head, the most northerly point in Scotland and 400 feet high, is a magnificent headland with some wonderful views including the cliffs of Orkney. Dunnet Bay and Dunnet Sands, known as the playground of Caithness, complete the coastline to Thurso.

Thurso

Status: Burgh.
How to Get There: (*By Air*). From Wick Airport. Weekday services to and from Inverness, Aberdeen, Edinburgh, Glasgow and London. Service to the Orkneys and Shetlands.
(*By Rail.*) Through trains to Aberdeen, Inverness, Edinburgh and London. Connections at Inverness for Kyle of Lochalsh.
(*By Road.*) During summer through bus services to Glasgow and Edinburgh. Excellent local services include Aberdeen and Inverness, with connections to the whole of Scotland.
Population: 9,400.
Early Closing Day: Thursday.
Post Office: Sinclair Street.
Tourist Information Centre: Riverside.
Places of Worship: Parish Church, St. Peter's, Princes Street. One or two other denominations have places of worship.
Parking Places: Riverside Road, junction of Sir George's Street and Riverside Road, Janet Street.
Cinema: Sir George's Street.
Parks and Open Spaces: St. John's Square.
Newspaper: Caithness Courier (Wednesday).
Other Amenities: Angling (Thurso River is one of the earliest salmon rivers in Scotland), good loch and sea fishing, bathing, boating bowls, golf, tennis, yachting, dancing.

THE BURGH OF THURSO is the most northerly town in Scotland and the port for the Orkney and Shetland Islands. It is a busy little town with a fairly modern harbour and salmon fishing in season.

Among the points of interest are the following. Thurso Castle of 1660, and the Castle of Scrabster, which sits on a lump of rock overlooking Scrabster Harbour. There is little left today but the situation is worth noting. The remains of Old St. Peter's Kirk. The oldest portions date from the thirteenth century while the south window is considered unique in Scottish medieval architecture. The Folk Museum in the Town Hall building. The Public Library and Museum. There are in addition a number of old houses and other interesting relics. One and a half miles off the road on the coast side, and six miles west of Thurso, is the very ancient Chapel of St. Mary's at Crosskirk, from where a pleasant walk along the coast towards Thurso will enable the visitor to see two brochs, an ancient chapel on the point of Brims Ness and Brims Castle ruins. Holborn Head, a short walk from Scrabster, is a magnificent and much broken headland with a wealth of caves and pot-holes.

A little before crossing the boundary into Sutherland there is a chambered cairn named Choc Freiceadain, in the care of the Dept. of Environment, one and a half miles east of Raey. Just on the Caithness side of the boundary is an Information Board which should prove very useful. The change in the countryside at the county boundary is remarkable. The road through Caithness follows fairly fertile land along the coast but, as soon as Sutherland is reached at the highest point the herbage is largely peat and heather, and continues so, getting more and more rugged towards the west. At one time this was all crofting country and suffered badly during the Clearances. Today there are a few crofts and some of the largest sheep-holdings in the country. At various points little lanes run down to the sea, usually past a croft, and since the coast is as scenic as it is possible to imagine these lanes are worth exploring. Just before the little village of Melvich the A897 leaves the main road and traverses Strath Halladale and Strath Kildonan, through some of the highest and loneliest of moorlands, to join the A9 at Helmsdale. Rather over half-way along this road a narrow road takes off to the west, through virtually uninhabited country, to Strathnaver, from where a left or right turn will rejoin the A836 at Altnaharra or Bettyhill.

At Tongue the A836 turns south between the magnificent Ben Loyal and Loch Loyal, through tremendous mountain country to Lairg, which is some seventeen miles from Dornoch. From Tongue the coast road continues along this most scenic of coasts, twisting and turning around the deep sea-lochs through a countryside that has the appearance of the Devil's Playground; here the bones of the earth are very close to the surface, and the soil, where there is any, is very thin, yet at every little river or burn, and this applies to the whole north coast of Sutherland, fertility exists and crofters or farmers are at work; many of the crofts are built alongside a tiny harbour, for once fishing was combined with crofting.

H

DURNESS AND THE SMOO CAVE

At Durness, the most north-westerly village in Scotland, a visit should
be made to the Smoo Cave, which is fascinating to a degree and
where there is a waterfall of 250 feet. Unfortunately it cannot be seen
but can be heard very plainly. South of Durness a ferry, and a
mini-bus will carry the visitor, for there is no through road, to Cape
Wrath, the most isolated spot in the British Isles and the highest cliffs.
Southwards from Durness the road cuts across to Rhiconich,
through a hard, wild land of rock and very little forest, the best of
which is between Rhiconich and Kinlochbervie, reached by a side-road
this is a nice little fishing village on a wonderful coast. The same
country and scenery continues to Laxford Bridge, where turn left for
one of the finest hill and loch-side roads in the Highlands to Lairg,
while the coast road follows the same magnificent coast and inland
scenery to Scourie and the ferry at Kylestrome for Kylesku across
Loch Glendhu. One mile south of the ferry turn right for Lochinver
and the finest scenery in Sutherland; a wild and upturned land of rock
but with many, many little green valleys, lochs and lochans, and all
close beside the sea on a very beautiful coast. Two very fine shapely
mountains have been in sight for some time, Quinag and Sail Ghorn.

LOCHINVER AND ASSYNT

The village of Lochinver is a delightful spot with a good fishing fleet,
good shops and a promenade along Loch Inver, a sea-loch. Here, in
the country known as Lochinver and Assynt, the country undergoes
another dramatic change as it gets greener, much less hard and wild
than Sutherland, but still with plenty of rock scenery and glorious
mountains, more heather and less bare rock. Near the eastern end
of Loch Assynt is Ardvreck Castle, almost in the shadow of that
upstanding mountain Suilven. Just across the Ross and Cromarty
boundary is the Inverpolly Nature Reserve, with a visitors' centre and
a fine viewpoint. Inverpolly has 26,000 acres with Red and Roe
Deer, Wild Cat, Pine Marten, Golden Eagle and Seals off-shore.
From Ledmore, a little north of the entrance to Inverpolly, the A837
strikes eastwards through the very beautiful Glen Oykel and Strath
Oykel to Bonar Bridge, traversing some of the lovliest scenery.
Southwards the A835 heads for Ullapool, passing several side-roads
towards the coast which are all worth exploring.

ULLAPOOL. Population 600.

Ullapool must be counted one of the most pleasant little places on
the west coast. It sits on a promontory jutting into Loch Broom, is a
major herring landing port and is the centre of a superb countryside,
with magnificent mountains and woods. Twelve miles south of the
village on the coast road are the Gorge of Corrieshalloch and the Falls
of Measach; the gorge is a mile long and 200 feet deep while the

falls plunge 150 feet to the bottom of the gorge. They are owned by the National Trust for Scotland. South of the Gorge the road, the A835, continues past Loch Glascarnoch, some fine hill country and open moorland, Loch Garve and the village of Contin to the Muir of Ord.

From the Gorge the A832 turns northwards to join the coast on the south of Loch Broom and follow it to Gruinard Bay, Loch Ewe and the Inverewe Gardens, which are in the hands of the National Trust for Scotland. These gardens, which were started in 1862, are an amazing achievement, for here grow semi-tropical plants and trees of many kinds on what was, a hundred years ago, little short of bare rock. Nearby is a Stage House, caravan site, and Information Centre, etc.

A few miles south of Poolewe is the village of Gairloch, the tourist centre for this part of Wester Ross. It has an enviable situation in the wide sweeping bay formed by Loch Gair, with a view west to the Hebrides and east to some of the finest Highland country. From Poolewe and Gairloch two side-roads run north to finish in little-known country. The A832 turns south-east from Gairloch to follow more than half of the banks of the beautiful Loch Maree and pass close by the Victoria Falls. At Kinlochewe the A832 continues eastwards to Glen Docherty, Loch a' Croisg and Achnasheen, from where a moorland journey with many beautiful spots finishes at the Muir of Ord.

From Kinlochewe the A896 passes the Beinn Eighe Nature Reserve and the 14,000-acre estate of the National Trust for Scotland. Known as the Torridon Estate, it includes some of the finest mountain scenery

The Gorge of Corrieshalloch near Ullapool

and rises to a height of over 3,000 feet. The road follows the River
Torridon, the banks of Loch Torridon and Loch Carron to the ferry
at Stromeferry, where the Strome Castle, National Trust, is well worth
viewing. From three miles north of Stromeferry the A890 runs through
very beautiful country along Glen Carron to Achnasheen. Once over
the ferry at Strome it is a short run to the Balmacara Estate, under the
National Trust, with an Information Centre in the village of Balmacara.
The Kyle of Lochalsh is four miles farther on and the port for
embarkation for Skye and the Hebrides. From Kyle of Lochalsh to
Fort William is about seventy miles of some of the finest scenery along
Loch Duich, with the lovely picture of the Castle of Eilean Donan, the
most beautiful situation of all the castles in Scotland, then along
Glen Shiel to Loch Garry and Invergarry, where the main Inverness–
Fort William road is joined. Close to the south-western end of Loch
Duich is the National Trust property of Kintail, which includes those
famous mountains the Five Sisters of Kintail. South of Lochalsh is
the mountainous, barely inhabited land of Knoydart, with no roads
and many lochs, magnificent country for the walker with experience
but not for the amateur. The next road to the south is the wonderful
run from Mallaig to Fort William.

MALLAIG. Population 849

Mallaig is the end of the road and the railway from Fort William; it is
also the end of 'The Road to The Isles'. Here at this busy fishing port
one may embark for many of the smaller islands as well as Stornoway
and the Kyle of Lochalsh, an extremely nice and popular resort in fine
Highland country. Many of the crofts around Loch Nevis have no
roads and are serviced by boat; this is one of the most enjoyable
experiences, to travel on these small diesel boats, with perhaps twenty
other passengers, around Loch Nevis, dropping mail and parcels at all
the crofts. Inland from Mallaig there is some fine walking in both
north and south Morar and farther inland in Lochaber; but be sure
you can use a map and compass, for this is wild country.

The road from Mallaig follows the coast past the Silver Sands of
Morar to Arisaig and Lochailort, where the A861 turns right to follow
the coast through the lovely lands of Moidart, Sunart, Ardnamurchan
and Morvern. This is a wonderful piece of country, cut up with lochs,
spattered with hills of 1,500 feet and more and bounded by the sea.
Loch Eilt, Loch Eil and Loch Linnhe. In this area there is a wealth of
old castles and scenery of the most beautiful kind in the Highlands.
At the eastern end of Glen Tarbert, at the village of Carron, the ferry
may be taken across the narrow neck of Loch Linnhe to the Fort
William road, which is only eight miles to the north.

From Lochailort the motorist could take the A830 along the Lochs
Eilt and Eil, passing Glenfinnan and the National Trust Monument to
the '45 Rising and Prince Charles Edward, and so into Fort William

by the direct route. This is one of the most scenic runs and closely
follows the railway, which is regarded as one of the most scenic in
Europe.

The Island of
Skye and The Hebrides

Since there are something like 500 islands in the Hebridean group it is
obviously impossible to deal with them all. Skye, Barra, South Uist,
North Uist, Benbecula, Harris and Lewis are the most popular in the
Hebridean group, and so will be dealt with here. The many smaller
islands should not be forgotten, and most can be reached by ferry
or hired boat, and all vary tremendously, from rich and fertile with a
wealth of wild flowers, to barren rocks above the sea; all have a
wealth of historical interest and many remains from the years long
before St. Columba, to the Viking invasions and subsequent Clans of
the twelfth to seventeenth centuries.

Skye is usually approached by ferry from the Kyle of Lochalsh,
which is connected by rail with Inverness and thus with London and
all important centres, as it is by coach services. The ferry takes but a
few minutes to Kyleakin. Skye can also be reached by steamer from
Mallaig, the landing port being Portree or Armadale. At Portree is the
Information Centre of the Isle of Skye Tourist Association.

On reaching Kyleakin two things at once come to the visitor's
notice: the Lighthouse Island, which is a Wildlife Park and open to the
public—tickets can be obtained from the Tourist Board's caravan in
Kyleakin—and the twelfth- or thirteenth-century castle at the entrance
to the harbour. Its name is Caisteal Maol, or the bald Castle, the castle
without battlements. The most prominent feature of Skye is the
Cuillin Hills, several of which rise to well over 3,000 feet and are
largely bare rock, with little vegetation, except in the valleys. It is their
outline when seen from a distance that gives these hills their great
attraction: the whole area of the Cuillins is quite remarkable in its
innate attraction, a mighty upthrust of bare rock with valleys and
gorges twisting between the various high points. This is climbing
country but there are one or two very fine walks, and a chat with the
police at Broadford will enable the newcomer to mark out a suitable
walk on a map; great care is needed when walking or climbing in the
south of Skye.

Northwards from Kyleakin the country is flat with the always
beautiful backcloth of hills which add a touch of magic to the most
uninteresting countryside. At Broadford there is a small bus which
leaves every morning for the coast south of the Cuillins and is a
great help to walkers and climbers. Sixteen miles north of Broadford
is the Sligachan Inn, at the head of the Sea Loch Sligachan and the
junction of the roads to Portree and Dunvegan.

North Skye is a very beautiful mixture of moorland, flat-topped hills and ragged cliffs and pinnacles, of tiny crofter villages, of old castles and reminders of the great Clans of days gone by. The most famous of these relics of the past is Dunvegan Castle, on Dunvegan Loch. Once a Highland castle with ramparts it is today a modern up-to-date mansion, but in the reconditioning has lost none of its character nor to a large extent its appearance. It is the world centre of the Clan MacLeod and inside are many treasures connected with the history of this Clan.

As compared to many of the mainland areas of the Highlands, Skye is sadly lacking in trees, but this is completely compensated for by the ground growth with a wealth of wild flowers in season. Near the coast is the machair, a particular kind of grassy and flower-studded verge to the sea-shore which often extends well inland. And the heather in the autumn is as fine as anywhere. A little west of Broadford are two tiny and very beautiful lochs. There are many more in the centre of Skye but few in the north; however, the magnificent coastline and the sea lochs have given Skye a reputation she richly deserves. The most northerly town is Uig, the embarkation point for the Western Isles.

The Isle of Lewis

Lewis is the largest and most northerly of the Western Isles, a term which should rightly be applied only to the Outer Hebrides. Its Gaelic name is Eilean an Fhraoich, which means the Island of Heather. Stornoway, towards the northern end of Lewis, is the only town in the Western Isles, and it is here that the steamers call. It is said locally that Stornoway is five towns in one, a market town, a manufacturing centre, the Island capital, a seaport and the centre of a very loyal overseas empire. Stornoway port is one of the best protected and can be entered in all weathers and all tides, and it is still a busy fishing port. Lewis is now connected with Glasgow by a regular air service.

The most outstanding feature of Lewis is the number of lochs and the lack of high hills, while the coastline, except in the far north, must be one of the most indented and broken in Scotland. The motor roads cover most of the island but there are still large areas where only the walker can go. Immediately across the island from Stornoway is the village of Carloway, near which is a very good sample of the broch, a type of Pictish fortified dwelling that can only be found in Scotland and dates from Roman times or a little before. Farther north at the village of Ballanthrushal is the Thrushel Stone, a 20-foot-high monolith, and farther north again is the lighthouse on the Butt of Lewis. On the west coast south of Carloway there is one of the finest stone circles near the village of Callanish; this is reputed to be one of the most perfect temples of its kind in the British Isles and may date from 2000 to 3000 B.C. The Island of Great Bernera, off the west coast, is connected by bridge with the mainland of Lewis. Near Carloway are two beaches with pure white sand, Dalmore and Dalbeg. On the south-east coast is the district of Park or Pairc, with a Deer Park Forest and herds of Red Deer. Lewis is an enchanting island with many picturesque villages, many ancient monuments, and much scenery of the finest kind, though not always Highland in topography.

The Isle of Harris

In fact Harris and Lewis are one island but the topography is completely different, and before there was a road the high hills on the boundary made a very definite border-line; so the two communities grew up in separate worlds and have always been distinct peoples even to the dialect of Gaelic spoken.

North Harris, which is joined to South Harris by the tiny neck of land at East and West Loch Tarbert, is a mountainous land dominated by the 2,600 feet of Clisham, surrounded by many lesser mountains and wild moorland. Only one motor road traverses it from north to south, with one side-road to Husinish, on the west coast close to the Island of Scarp; so that among these mountains, many of them are over 2,000 feet, is fine walkers' country with many miles of sparsely inhabited, loch dotted countryside that requires map and compass for safe navigation.

Many remains have been found on Harris from 2,000 years ago and some of these are semi-permanent and can be seen in the form of stone forts or duns; there is a very fine one at Rodel near the southern point of Harris. South Harris is almost entirely a crofting island as it was before the Clearances in the early nineteenth century; it is also a good deal less rugged than North Harris. Both have an irresistible attraction which springs as does the attraction of all the west coast islands, from a combination of fine scenery, the closeness of the sea, the sense of timelessness and lack of the need to hurry plus the history of the Clans which has been much dramatised in song and story. However, no matter what this attraction is based on it is there, and a visit does nothing to dispel it but rather confirms it.

Leverburgh, in the south-west corner of South Harris, is a reminder of Lord Leverhulme's great attempt to industrialise these islands in the early years of this century. Beyond the village named after him is the promontory of Toe Head, with fine cliffs and nesting grounds for many sea-birds, including Fulmars; there is an ancient chapel which was probably built around the same time as St. Clement's at Rodel. Chaipaval is the high point of this promontory, which looks straight out into the Atlantic, and from its summit is one of the finest views obtainable anywhere, the hills of North Uist, the Cuillins of Skye and fifty miles to the west, the stacs of St. Kilda; all these can be seen with miles of the rolling Atlantic.

The south coast of North Harris and the west coast of South Harris have many fine beaches of sand with a background of machair and a final backcloth of hills; in the summer these are beautiful coasts but in winter few lands have the same fury of the Atlantic to contend with. The high and steep cliffs overlooking West Loch Tarbert are said to be the haunt of the Golden Eagle, as well as the Raven and many other mountain birds.

North Uist

On the map North Uist looks like a jigsaw puzzle and must contain as much water, in the form of lochs, as land. Lochmaddy is the port and the only village of importance. The east coast consists of mountains and lochs, with far more of the latter and all good trout fishing. The west coast is flat machair land, fertile and well cropped, and tulips are grown commercially. The coast consists of miles of silver sands with, as a rule, only the sea-birds to disturb the peace. This is an island with more relics of the days of prehistory than most, and will prove a happy hunting ground for the archaeologist and historian, as well as for the holidaymaker seeking peace and relief from the rush and tear of city life.

Benbecula

The small island of Benbecula lies between North and South Uist and is now connected to both by causeway and bridge. There are on the west side moorland and heather which slopes down to the machair land, which is cultivated as in North Uist, and here again are miles and miles of silvery sands. The east coast is a maze of lochs and islands with one or two hills approaching a thousand feet. At Bramsdale, at the southern end of the causeway to North Uist, is an Information Centre for tourists. At Bailivanich is the airport, a garage and a bus service to Lochboisdale in South Uist. This small island is one that should afford great pleasure to the explorer on foot who does not wish for the rough going of the hills and mountains.

South Uist

South Uist consists of three separate regions. The west coast is largely sandy beaches backed by flowering machair land, the centre is mostly fresh water lochs and peat, and the east coast consists of mountains, a few up to 2,000 feet, with much more rugged scenery and a broken coastline with many long indentations and sea lochs, three of which conceal the three ports of Loch Skiport, Loch Eynort and Lochboisdale. In the village of Eochdar is the Black House Museum, which contains much that is most interesting of island life in the past; the Black House is itself of even greater interest.

There are, perhaps, more species of birds on South Uist than anywhere else, and at Stilligary is a Nature Reserve. There is a road which runs eastward through the Reserve to Loch Skiport, and from this much of the wild life can be seen. Lochboisdale is the port of embarkation from the mainland.

Isle of Barra

Barra has been called the Garden of the Hebrides and can claim over a thousand varieties of flowers. It is a very small island; the road which encircles it is only fifteen miles long but it includes some of the most beautiful scenery in the Hebrides.

Cockle Strand, a two-mile square of sand, firm and hard at low tide, is the landing ground for the daily flight which connects Barra with the outside world. The best beaches are at Tangusdale, Allasdale and Vaslane, while of hills there are many with a few over the thousand feet. The easy climb to the summit of Heaval is rewarded with a magnificent view of Barra Head, the Cuillins of Skye, Canna, Rhum and Eigg. The walk from Cliat to Vaslane past the Clait Caves is a particularly pleasant one, and at Ardmhor the colony of seals will be seen. Both sea angling and loch fishing is a speciality and is well catered for.

In order to gain a full appreciation of the Hebrides, and their attractions are many and varied, their beauties simple and heart-warming, the visitor must take a timeless tour, not a rushed two-day trip. Come to the islands with the intention of quietly exploring and forget the clock for the duration of the holiday.

Eilean Donan Castle

Kirkwall

Status: City and Royal Burgh.
How to Get There: (*By Air*). Daily Service from Wick, Inverness, Edinburgh and Glasgow Airports to Kirkwall.
(*By Sea.*) Daily sailings from Scrabster (Thurso) to Stromness. Bus service Kirkwall. There are also sailings from Aberdeen to Kirkwall. Sailing days and times should be ascertained in advance.
Population: 18,500.
Early Closing Day: Wednesday.
Post Office: Junction Road.
Tourist Information Office: Orkney Tourist Organisation, Mounthoolie Lane.
Places of Worship: Episcopalian, St. Magnus Cathedral. Presbyterian. A few other denominations have places of worship.
Parking Places: Junction Road, Mill Street, Great Western Road.
Cinema: Phoenix Cinema, Junction Road.
Theatre: Orkney Arts Theatre, Mill Street.
Parks and Open Spaces: Pickaquoy Park, Bignold Park, Brandyquoy Park.
Newspaper: Orcadian (Thursday).
Other Amenities: Although all the usual amenities may be found here it is as the base from which to explore for the unusual that Kirkwall excels.

WITHIN THE CONFINES of this Guide it is not possible to do justice to the Orkney Islands. Although Kirkwall is a suitable place for the ordinary holiday it excels as the base from which to explore for the unusual in Scotland's history and scenery.

St. Magnus Cathedral at Kirkwall is an outstanding example of a Scottish cathedral dating from the twelfth century. The Bishop's Round Tower, the Earl's Palace and many other buildings of ancient lineage if of lesser importance are to be found in this very fascinating city.

The Orkneys consist of about a hundred islands north and south of the mainland island. Almost every one is rich in historic remains of life in the Orkneys from prehistory to the present century, from the Ring of Brogar, a remarkable set of Standing Stones, to Scapa Flow and the Churchill Barrier. The prehistoric village of Skara Brae is an outstanding example. Scenery and the bird life is tremendous and continually varying, from the Old Man of Hoy to the finest bathing beaches in peace and quiet well away from the crowds that frequent the better-known resorts farther south. If you visit the Orkneys do so with an open mind and leave your watch at home; go to explore and enjoy the long days that in June are nearly twenty-four hours in length, the sense of space and freedom from restrictions imposed by modern city life, the birds, the wild life and the remarkable coast scenery that in places is outstanding; and the quite remarkable relics of the past in these very beautiful islands where time does not seem to matter, where music does matter in the crofts and the little homes of the islanders, where the simple delights still have a value and the harassed city-dweller can be refreshed.

Lerwick

Status: Royal Burgh.
How to Get There: (*By Air*). Service from London, Birmingham, Manchester, Glasgow, Edinburgh, Aberdeen, Inverness, Wick and Orkney.
(*By Sea.*) Sailings from Aberdeen and Kirkwall.
Sailing days and times should be ascertained in advance.
Population: 6,500.
Early Closing Day: Wednesday.
Post Office: The Harbour.
Tourist Information Centre: Shetland Tourist Organisation, Alexandra Wharf.
Places of Worship: Parish Church, St. Columba's, Church of Scotland. A few other denominations have places of worship.
Parking Places: Varied and plentiful.
Cinema: The North Star, Harbour Street.
Theatre: The Garrison Theatre.
Parks and Open Spaces: Gilbertson Park, King George V Park.
Newspaper: Shetland Times (Friday).
Other Amenities: While Lerwick is a holiday resort in its own right it is as the centre from which to explore the islands of the group that Lerwick excels. Most sports are represented and all the usual amenities are to hand.

THE ZETLAND OR SHETLAND ISLES are the most northerly in the British Isles; the most southerly is about thirty miles north of the northernmost point of the Orkneys while the Zetlands themselves, from south to north, are about thirty-five miles in length. The most northerly is thus not far short of a thousand miles from London. This fact is realised best in June when daylight is almost continuous throughout the twenty-four hours. The other natural phenomena of the

Zetlands is the almost complete absence of trees. There is said to be one plantation only on the many scores of islands comprising the Zetlands.

This, above any part of Scotland, is the land of brochs, the land where these almost prehistoric dwellings can be seen most frequently, as well as Pictish settlements, cairns and burial mounds from times long before the Vikings invaded these lovely islands. Of all parts of Scotland invaded by those pirates the Shetlands and the Orkneys have retained most from that period, their populations being today very largely Scandinavian in origin.

Knitting and music are two of the delights of these islands, while tweed is still woven on hand-looms. While Lerwick and Scalloway are two of the most fascinating towns, with much to show the visitor, it is the countryside and more especially the coast that is the main attraction of the Zetlands. The herds of wild Shetland ponies are an added attraction, as are the amazing variety of sea birds, for in the Zetlands you cannot get away from the sea; the islands are narrow and stretch northwards in a narrow belt so that the sea has always dictated life and its comings and goings throughout the ages. For the archaeologist and historian, for those after the unusual holiday, for the lover of nature or for those who just want relief from the cares of town life with the continuous crowds, make the trip to the Zetland Isles and see what you will find. The last line can very well be applied to the whole of the more remote areas of the Highlands and Islands of Scotland.

In Glen Ogle

Index